KITES

For Everyone

How to Make and Fly Them

MARGARET GREGER

Diagrams by
DEL GREGER

Dover Publications, Inc., Mineola, New York

Acknowledgements

In a book such as this it is always difficult to give due credit. I am indebted to many generous kitemakers. The dedication in my first book, *Blown Sky-High*, was to "kitemakers, past and present, who have shared their work so generously . . . all the way back to unknown Oriental kitemakers." All of us who make kites are aware of the many hands that preceded ours. Throughout the book I mention various kite designers in connection with the kites which they developed. The list includes Guy Aydlett, A. van Breda, Leonard Conover, Tony Cyphert, Ed Grauel, Gary Hinze, Bill Lee, Joseph Lee, John Loy, Carol Master, Joan Newcomb, Stephen Robinson, Francis Rogallo, Scott Spencer, John Spendlove, Steve Sutton, and Lee Toy.

My own work would not have been possible without the pupils and the teachers in the various schools where, over a period of twenty years, I learned to be the Kite Lady. These include the children and teachers of the Richland, Washington, School District and of Educational Service District 123; the children, board, and staff of Chief Joseph Summer Seminars, Wallowa County, Oregon; and Jack and Frances Ehrig of Locust Grove Press, who printed my earlier books.

Angela Dittmar, Bob Ingraham, Tom Sisson, Bill Tyrrell, Jack Van Gilder, and Vi and Elmo Weeks are also among those who helped. Vi Weeks and Debora Greger read the manuscript. Vi made several of the fabric kites, vetting the patterns. Many hands have worked on the drawings including Joan Newcomb, Pierr Morgan, and Del, Debora, and Greg Greger.

Debora oversaw this third edition, and it would not have happened without her. Kelly Barber of Gainesville, Florida, brought her formatting and typesetting skills to the task of putting it all together.

Bibliographical Note

This Dover edition, first published in 2006, is a slightly corrected republication of the third edition of *Kites for Everyone,* originally published by the author in Richland, Washington, in 2000. The "Resources" section has been updated for this edition.

International Standard Book Number

ISBN-13: 978-0-486-45295-1
ISBN-10: 0-486-45295-6

Manufactured in the United States by LSC Communications
45295608   2018
www.doverpublications.com

Today
I saw the Kitemaker
Testing the results
Of her handiwork,
Tossing
Them out one by one
Into the winds
Of the future,
Tethered
Only by the fragile
Strings of her love
To the world she knows.

Tomorrow
She will give
Into the hands of others
Kites bearing her mark
Wondering
Will they fly,
Or be flown,
Steady or storm-whipped,
Hoping
The colors of earth,
Buoyant and beautiful,
Will enhance the sky.

—*Virginia Horton*

Contents

Introduction

Kites for Everyone—a running start for beginning kitemakers, with, thanks to generous kite designers, such beauties as the Facet and the Flowform to challenge the experienced. When I wrote *Blown Sky-High: Kites for the Classroom,* in 1977, my first aim was to bring all my notes, patterns and lists between covers in a convenient form for my kitemaking classes and workshops. Sooner or later, almost every kitemaker is invited to help a class, a Cub Scout den, or a Sunday School group make kites, and *Blown Sky-High* was welcomed. I had already overseen the production of thousands of classroom kites, and the book was based on the solid experience that falling into all possible pitfalls gives. It was reviewed in library journals and school arts magazines and was soon in libraries and schools all over the country. Kite shops came to rely on it as the answer to "Can you show me how to make kites with my fourth grade class?"

In 1979, *More Simple Kites* combined some new favorites with kites which came to me from people who had used *Blown Sky-High* and who wrote, "Would you like to see the kite I make in my daughter's pre-school class?"

Simple Fabric Kites, 1982, was written to make kitemaking accessible to competent home sewers. For the most part, the available instructions for cloth kites had been written by kitemakers who were inventing sewing as they went along. My contribution was translating kitemaking into standard sewing terms and simplifying and sequencing the sewing steps.

Kites For Everyone, 1984, combined these three books with much new material. By 1990, I had found still other great kites, enough for a second book, *More Kites For Everyone,* with 17 more kites which ranged from simple to challenging.

Now it's 2000 and time to revise *Kites For Everyone* before I reprint. The old classics remain but, in the interim, new materials which simplify kitemaking have come along and more kite favorites have joined the crowd.

Using This Book

Kites For Everyone is organized according to kite types, a chapter for deltas, one for sleds, and so on. In a single chapter, the kites will range from a 15-minute bag kite costing about 25¢ to a fabric kite which may take several hours to construct at a cost of several dollars. This organization emphasizes the diversity possible with a single design, and kitemakers, who know well that one thing leads to another, will appreciate the range of options.

In the way we talk about kites, and in the way prizes are distributed at kite contests, it may seem that fabric kites are considered in some sense "better" and plastic and paper kites "inferior." Simplicity and low cost do not imply inferiority. My own preference is for the 15-minute wonder, and, in this collection, I am particularly proud of the classroom kites, many of which use a plastic or high-density polyethylene bag as a module. Kitemakers should look at a shopping bag as Michelangelo looked at a block of marble.

I built my first kite, a two-stick diamond, of willow poles and brown wrapping paper, over sixty years ago. There was not much to read about kites in Western Nebraska in the thirties, and our materials were also limited, sticks split from orange crates, kraft paper from mail order packages. My husband built his first two-stick kites to fly frame forward, and learned what was wrong only when he saw a store-bought kite. Today's kitemakers can begin with good patterns and materials and have a broad range of kite designs to choose from.

Various options for bridle, tails and other finishing details are shown for each kite design. Available materials, prevailing winds and personal preference determine choices. Most kitemakers come to have a favorite kite design, generally one which does well in the local winds. But we all like to try something new, even if it only reaffirms our loyalties. In a sense, the patterns are like a standard recipe. With the correct proportions of yeast, flour and liquid, and an understanding of the principles, you can make almost any kind of bread.

Classroom Kites

Since 1969, I have been teaching kitemaking and kiteflying in elementary and secondary classrooms, in college classes, in summer camps, and in workshops for adults and families. The workshops are a short kite course in which several kites are built, using various materials and construction methods, thus giving the students experience with different designs and techniques. Kites provide inexpensive, exciting leads into many areas–art, crafts, engineering, math and even history, since the development of kites is traced in both East and West. They are also simply fun–an activity to be shared by all ages. They are for poets, inventors and all of us who like to hold our work in our hands and watch it take off into the sky.

How do I feel about Charlie Brown and his kite? About his chronic, predestined failure to fly a kite? I don't like it, that's how. Kites should be a symbol not of failure but of soaring, spirit-freeing success. I've overseen the making of a few thousand kites in my "career" as a teacher of kitemaking. There was one, a Siamese Snake not that carefully made, which I could not get to fly–and that on a day when eighty third-graders were flying eighty Snakes. But that was not failure. I said, "We can take care of this. We'll frame another face, put this tail on it, and come back out and fly."

We should set up the classroom situation to insure success. Sufficient time and good work space are essential. Kite teachers also need to eliminate such phrases as "You did that wrong" or "You made a mistake." Remember that almost anything can be made to fly and that there are not many kites with only one "right" way. Because I don't want to spend an hour working out bridling systems for thirty ill-made kites, I stress precision and care–and work with tolerant kite designs.

Several of our school buildings have three linked classrooms forming a "pod." In one school, the teachers wanted to have all three of the sixth-grade classes make the kites at once. Eighty-seven students were involved. I first met with the three classroom teachers, the librarian and the principal, and made the kite, the Siamese Snake, with them. Two days later, we set up supply tables and sample kites in each class area, to spread the action out. Everybody gathered around to watch me make a kite. The students then went back to their desks to begin work while the adults circulated to advise, remind, and ward off mistakes. It was hectic, but worth it because the wind was ideal and, at the close of the afternoon, we had scores of Snakes in the air at once.

Classroom Kite Criteria

♦   **They must be winners.** We don't want to teach people that kites are hard to make and really don't fly very well.

♦   **They must use easily-obtainable, inexpensive materials.** This is relative. The Oriental kites are framed with matchstick bamboo reed, which, if you will all forgive me, doesn't grow on trees, at least not in Washington State. But when you find a reed blind you have material for hundreds of kites.

♦   **They must be completed in about an hour** so the kite can be finished and perhaps flown on the day it is made.

Even though kites are one of the world's oldest toys, many adults also need confidence-building in order to attempt to make or to fly a kite. One of the great side benefits of successful classroom kitemaking is the feeling of competence and the confidence which competence confers. Mistakes are rarely fatal errors. A spar snaps, we replace it; paper tears, we patch or re-cover; string breaks, and we may mourn the loss, but we also cheer the brief flight in freedom and turn to build another. As we adjust bridles and bows to suit the wind of the day, shorten or lengthen tails, and trim for balance, we learn to *observe* how the kite flies, *diagnose* a problem and *prescribe* a remedy.

The Vietnamese Kite is inexpensive, easy and so tolerant it will fly even if it is bridled upside down. One summer at the sidewalk art show where I was selling kites and books, a nine-year-old boy whose mother was selling photographs spent much of the show's first day flying a Little Delta which I had laid out as a "test kite." Early the next morning he asked hesitantly if I would consider trading a book for a photograph–trades among artists being one of the pleasurable benefits of participating in a crafts show. Kevin was fearful I would say no but I told him I would be by to close a deal. I traded two books and some matchstick bamboo reed for a fine photograph of the Arizona desert, and Kevin stopped flying my kite and disappeared. Soon he was back to see if I had a ruler. No ruler, but a paper cutter to trim his piece of newspaper to 12"x12". Then he borrowed glue, followed by crepe paper tail streamers. I was demonstrating the Vietnamese and had invited him to watch, but he just smiled and kept borrowing. Finally, he brought his own Vietnamese Kite around for help with the bridle–and string to fly it. It was an occasion of total pride for all of us.

Lee Wilbur used the Dutch Kite in his first grade classroom. When he called to invite me to come see what he was doing, I remonstrated, "Lee, the Dutch Kite is hard! There are so many skills involved: folding, cutting, gluing, knots. I don't make that kite in first grade unless I have a helper for every three students."

"Well," he said, "we have a 15-minute activity period every day. The first day we fold, the second day we glue, and by the end of the week, we are out on the football field flying kites." The class had been making Dutch Kites for two weeks when I went to see them. They could make kites on their lunch hour, they could repair kites, they understood bridling a two-stick kite. They glowed with competence–all by means of a 12"x16" sheet of butcher paper, some glue and a little string.

Nowadays, my kite evangelism is done in teacher workshops and in talks to groups of teachers and librarians. Here, I spread the word that I have patterns, bibliographies and scarce materials (matchstick bamboo reed in these parts) available free or at my cost. My real goal in all this is not more kites or even better kites but competent kids, people who know that the work of their hands will fly.

Things to Consider

♦ **The time:** I always try to negotiate an hour and a half for a class, time for cleanup–and for flying, if the day permits. If kitemaking classes are back-to-back it is essential to have time to straighten the supplies and tools between sessions. If flying is on the schedule, make it clear at the beginning that early finishers help the others and cleanup precedes flying.

In an hour you can make a plastic or paper kite and clean up afterwards. An hour-and-a-half allows time for flying if site and weather permit. If flying is planned, check the site for safety. Allow time before class to arrange the furniture, set up the supply table, and distribute tools, patterns, and materials to individual tables. Anyone who walks in early can help.

♦ **General:** Encourage helpers. Say yes when asked, "Can I help with the next class?" (Check with the teacher first.) Some of us need all the help we can get when knot time comes. Aides keep materials organized, find tools, and give a hand as needed. They can carry kitemaking to future classes.

♦ **The local climate:** (dry or moist) and the wind of the day may determine the choice between paper and plastic kites, and between sled and delta designs. Paper absorbs moisture and the weight of the kite can increase dramatically if humidity is high.

♦ **The working space:** Making kites takes room. Fellow staffers have suggested that this kitemaker is happy only when she has all the tables, all the scissors, and everyone else out of the way.

♦ **Discouraging dependence:** If you give a demo and post a sample kite and brief instructions, and then jump in to do it again at the first "What do I do now?" all is lost. Confidence evaporates. Refer kids to the sample, to the instructions, to a neighbor who is proceeding correctly. Interfere and take over only to prevent disaster.

♦ **Be prepared:** Insist that this is not a tree-climbing or a rock-throwing class. With any class, odds are that at least one kite may come to rest in a tree or on a building. Cut the line as close to the tree as possible. If the kite has not been wedged in the tree by tugging, there's a good chance the wind may catch it and fly it out. Kites on roofs have been freed the same way. Breakaways are another matter. If the line is not tied to the reel or a sudden gust breaks the line, the kite is off and away. I call it a flight to freedom, rather than cause for grief. "You made that kite in less than an hour. You can make another in half an hour."

Preparing for a Class

At the beginning of each set of instructions is a materials list and a tools list. A quick rundown of these checklists will show whether the necessities are on hand.

When I am getting acquainted with a new kite and before I introduce it in the classroom, I make half a dozen and also test some variations. A snap swivel from the sporting goods store facilitates changing the reel from one kite to another when I test.

♦ **Age and size of group:** Age and ability determine how much help is needed. Err on the side of too many helpers. An extra adult or two does no harm and forwards the goal of broadening the pool of kite teachers. For K-3, a helper at each table is the minimum. Fifth and sixth graders who have already made the kite are worth their weight in gold. Generally, the people requesting the class should arrange for helpers. For adults and children over ten, twenty-five is a reasonable class size, if working space is adequate. I usually provide masking tape and a marking pen for nametags so we can all get acquainted before we begin work.

♦ **Team building:** Teams of two has much to recommend it. Sometimes this is dictated by the space. But even such small kites as the Siamese Snake are easier to frame with four hands than with two. Ten-year-olds can build the Bullet Kite by working on both sides of the table. Making two kites, one right after the other, consolidates the learning as initial awkwardness is overcome and the sequence becomes familiar.

♦ **Work Space:** Good work space is essential. Plan a square yard of table space for each kitemaker, plus a separate table for supplies. There are kites in this book small enough to be made at a desk, but tables facilitate sharing supplies and tools and even out skill levels as people help each other. If work must be done on the floor, move the desks out of the way. If tables are available, move the chairs because short arms have better leverage from a standing position. Cover the tables. Markers, glue, even stray bits of tape, can leave a mess. Provide good ventilation when markers are being used.

♦ **Tools:** Be sure to provide enough tools–pencils, scissors, tape and gluestick–to enable people to work efficiently without waiting for essentials. Bright ribbons or yarn tied to special tools help to keep track of them and to identify *my* tools. Fat tin cans on each table make handy tool organizers.

♦ **Scisssors:** Long, painful experience with school scissors led me to buy a dozen pairs of inexpensive scissors from an office supply house. Lengths of ribbon tied on the handles identify them as mine, first, and as good scissors, second. Lefthanders can use them readily, something to check if you plan to invest in class scissors. Workers should not have to put up with tools which make good results nearly impossible. Cutting tape makes scissor blades sticky. They can be cleaned with nail polish remover or other solvent. Again, good ventilation is necessary.

♦ **Glue:** I prefer gluestick to other adhesives for kitemaking because it is non-toxic and easily shared. White glue is slow to dry but satisfactory, except on tissue paper.

◆ **You bring the supplies.** What is clear to you as you describe a needed item on the phone can be something else entirely to the person who's never seen it and doesn't quite know how it will be used.

I always plan to have plenty of materials with an array of colors. The best way to discourage creativity is to be chintzy with supplies. I never tolerate waste, aimless slashing of materials, or fencing with dowels. But I want people to be able to come back for seconds and thirds, to make kites for mothers and little sisters, and to experiment with design variations after they have succeeded with a proven design. Stunning kites can be made of brown paper bags and newspaper. They are in no way inferior to creations of mylar. Whatever materials you have, have plenty. Working with abundance is stimulating.

◆ **Bamboo:** Window blinds made of matchstick bamboo reed supply the framing material for small Oriental kites. They are sold by some kite shops, by import shops, and may be found in thrift shops. Not all the reeds are uniform or strong enough for a Vietnamese or Snake Kite. Rejects are useful for strengthening the Dutch Kite and sparring some of the small bag kites. One-eighth, 3/16", and 1/4" diameter wooden dowels are the spar material for most of the small-to-medium-size kites in this book. Look for them in hardware and craft shops or in quantity from suppliers listed in the resource list.

◆ **Paper:** Most kitemakers are familiar with tissue paper and butcher paper. Art tissue comes in dozens of bright colors. From my newspaper, I save colored pages and pages with printing or illustrations which, trimmed to 12" square, would make attractive kite faces. At one summer camp, we made potato prints on newsstock and these, in turn, made elegant kites. Our import shop sometimes has Chinese newspapers which come as packing material. They can be ironed smooth and the graceful characters seem particularly fitting for Oriental kites. One of the most attractive collections of Dutch Kites I have seen was made of white butcher paper, painted with broad, wavy, black stripes before it was cut up and made into kites.

◆ **Plastic:** Several of these patterns use the "tall kitchen trash bag" as a module. Look for about 1 mil or less in thickness. Some bags are lighter to the point of being flimsy and, when kids and tape are involved, can be hard to handle. High-density polyethylene is the crackly plastic used in many shopping bags. It is tough and also suitable for kitemaking. Some materials may be difficult to find, but plastic bags are ubiquitous. If good colors are not available, I use white, which always looks good and can be decorated with permanent marking pens. Bags in many colors are available by mail and kite shops sometimes sell them.

Materials

◆ **One-eighth inch diameter dowels** are available in hardware and craft stores.

◆ **Cellophane tape** in 1/2" and 3/4" widths is used for assembling plastic kites. Small amounts of strapping and filament tape in the same widths reinforce tie-ons and spar attachments. In order to keep things moving, have two or three rolls of cello tape for each table. A single roll of strapping tape can be placed on the finishing table. **Self-adhesive labels** are an excellent alternative to strapping tape for spar and spreader attachment and tie-ons. They can be cut to size, usually in half, and handed out on the backing paper to the class. Labels are a wonderful alternative to rolls of tape.

♦ **Scrap plastic** is the usual choice for tails and gives the class experience in slicing plastic. Bright colored surveyors' tape can be used for tails. Kite shops which sell kitemaking materials stock most of these items. See the resource list.

Figure the cost of supplies, add a little for scrounging costs and give the organizer a unit cost for the project. Classroom kites cost 25¢ to 50¢ each. Even when the kites are made for a cause which I fully support and plan to donate to, I figure the costs and have the sponsors pay for materials. This is just good kite accounting. Organizations should know that kites are not expensive and can be included in future plans.

♦ **You bring the string.** For most of my kitemaking career my recommendation for flying line for classroom kites was #20 or #30 crochet thread. It is tough, not fuzzy, slow to tangle, inexpensive and was sold in large balls in most fabric shops. For just a few cents per kitemaker, you could have individual winders for class flying. However, the doily makers who were the primary consumers are disappearing and so is the market and the thread. Thrift shops may have it by the bagful. The heavier "bedspread crochet thread" is still available and may be the best solution, meeting the criteria of inexpensive, easy to find and easy to use. Asking each kitemaker to bring flying line can result in a wonderful assortment of unsuitable line, ranging from knitting yarn to chalk line. Use your judgment and test what you find. Ordinary thread is hard to handle. It can be sprayed with WD-40 to reduce tangling.

♦ **Corrugated cardboard** is cut into six-inch squares for the winders. First tie the string to the card. Failure to do this is a learning experience. The kite will just keep going after it takes out all the line. One hundred wraps puts fifty feet on the card, plenty for a first flight. Nothing beats the satisfaction of teacher and kitemaker as the kite is put to the test, even if it's only a turn around the gymnasium. *It flies, it really flies!!* Sections of heavy mailing tube, tin cans with both ends removed or notched boards also make inexpensive small winders. The bigger around–within reason–the less winding at reel-in time, a strong argument for furnishing something besides pencils and rulers.

Look around the classroom for **bridle measuring aids**. One wrap around a small table may give the five feet needed for the Siamese Snake kite. One and a half times around the work table could be nine feet for a large sled. Shorter bridles may use body measurements. An adult arm is about two feet and an adult "wing-span" about five feet.

♦ **Darning needles** are useful for bridling some kites. Store them in a block of styrofoam. When knives are used, protect the tables with scrap wood cutting boards.

Kitemaking Time

Hang a sample kite and, for some designs, samples of various stages of construction on the bulletin board. I make a step-by-step clue sheet for the kite-of-the-day. What comes first, what comes next. Tape one on each table and most of the "What do we do next?" questions are taken care of. Establish a finish-up site on a corner of the supply table or on a separate table. This is where one-time-use tools and supplies, such as strapping tape, craft knives and punches, and the string for bridles and flying line should remain. As you demonstrate, step to the finish table for the last steps, explaining how important it is for the shared tools to remain there. In the excitement of kitemaking, tools can sink without a trace.

Class: Open with a fifteen-minute demonstration, with everyone gathered around. As I work, I explain how a kite flies, tell the history of this particular kite, and harp on craftsmanship and the accompanying necessity for good tools, well cared for.

Demonstration: Begin with a short lecture. Include a little history, a hint of science, and a look at the kite-of-the-day. Explain how the class will be conducted, that is, a demonstration first, then orderly distribution of supplies, followed by kitemaking, clean–up, reel preparation, and flying. Stress that this is not a race. We want well-made kites we can be proud of. Flying begins only when construction is finished and the work space clean. Emphasize safety with particular reference to local flying sites. Talk about the judgment necessary for responsible kiteflying, mentioning busy streets and overhead wires by name. If you know of good flying sites in the neighborhood, recommend them.

Make a kite "before their very eyes." Choose a light color with contrasting trim or reinforcement, so the action shows clearly for the whole class. Demonstrate how to cut plastic and dowels. *Don't cut dowels with scissors!* Tape the demonstration kite up as a reference, designate a helper and ask the class to line up for supplies. A box for usable scraps for tails and decorations and a trash can for the scraps facilitates cleanup.

Following the demo, students receive materials from the supply table and move to the work tables. It helps to have someone at the supply table to hand out supplies during the initial "feeding frenzy." As work progresses, I circulate, field questions, and try to insure against fatal errors. For something of general interest, I raise my voice and tell the class. When it comes time to set a bridle, I stop the action and show everyone—for the second time. Those who finish first help others or wind line on the reels so we are all ready to fly at once.

Clean-up: Almost as soon as the demonstration is over and supplies distributed, Early Finishers are asking, "What now?" Be prepared. They can help others. Clean-up and reel preparation are other pre-flying tasks. Check all kites before they go out the door. If the kite bridle must be reset, I will do that, holding it up to demonstrate a good flying stance and explaining what happens if the flying angle is incorrect.

Flying

Always check out the flying sites before going into the classroom. We don't want to teach children that it's all right to fly kites near power lines and busy streets.

Flying our kites and making the necessary adjustments and repairs brings the class from "This kite won't fly" to "What should I do so this kite will fly?" On the flying field, I stand in one place, looking resourceful. As I help adjust bridles, make tail recommendations, or deepen the bow on an Eddy Kite, I point out the flight characteristics of the kites in the air and those struggling to get in the air, suggesting reasons for varying performance. The emphasis is on careful observation. Soon we have several qualified kite technicians and I become the keeper of the field repair kit which should include scissors, knife, extra spars, tape, string and tail material.

Arts and Crafts

"It flies!" Exciting words in any language. Tal Streeter writes of "the kite smile... as the wind transforms the kite into an entity pulsing with life."

A kite *must* fly and, to some of us, all kites are beautiful, but the students in a junior high arts and crafts class where I spent a month, set out to go beyond utility to the stunning, the dramatic, the humorous. Emphasis was on fine appearance in the hand or in the air. Because beginning with a proven design facilitates improvisation, students first made the demonstrated kite–a different one each week. If someone wished to join the group later on, she could find an experienced builder to help her. Sudents were soon back for seconds and thirds, were teaching each other, and building kites to answer questions. Dutch Kite: "What will happen if I trim the bottom corners?" Flies, but not as well since lifting surface is reduced. Snake Kite: "If I cut the tail to ribbons?" Glorious variation, the octopus kite; teacher is stunned. Eddy Kite: "If I make tissue paper windows and glue fringe all around?" A beauty!

The inventiveness of each helped spark the imagination of all. Some brought their dreams to school, "I was flying my Snake after I went to sleep last night and it had a notched tail like a dragon."

Kitemakers become relaxed about mistakes and mishaps. As we bent the crosspiece to bow an Eddy Kite which Shannon had spent three days building, the stick snapped. I felt the whole class go tense, because the possibility that this kite–fashioned with great care and enthusiasm–might never fly, was plain before us. But I could smile and say, "It's serious, but it's not fatal," and hear Shannon exhale as I showed how to cut away the lashing at the center, slip the broken stick out of the framing cord, and replace it with a whole one.

After these classes ended, three of the students accompanied me to a first-grade class to help thirty-six six- and seven-year-olds make and fly the Dutch Kite. My assistants were impressed that skills which they now took for granted were so difficult to master.

History

1976, when I was Ye Olde Bicentennial Kitemaker in the Richland School District, was a great season of classroom kitemaking because it led me to biographies and autobiographies of those well-known North American inventors and kitemakers, U.S. Founding Father Benjamin Franklin and Canadian Alexander Graham Bell.

Our kite designs come from all over the world, but the Asian contribution is fundamental. I have put together what I call a Clothesline Kite Museum, a collection of forty kites, hung in chronological order on a line stretched across a classroom wall. Each has a card listing its provenance, with dates, inventors, and such uses as the French Military for observation, the Eddy and Hargraves for weather kites, and the parafoil for lifting and observations. The collection is for handling, and, after I talk my way through it and answer questions, students can take the kites down for a closer look.

Science and Math

One spring, I spent several weeks with a class of sixth-graders, building and testing kites for performance and gathering data for comparisons. We made simple wind gauges and clinographs for measuring altitude. As we discussed the physics of flight and the technological uses of kites, we were delighted to learn that before construction of the suspension bridge at Niagara Falls began, the first line across the gorge was carried by a boy's kite.

We built Dutch, Eddy and Sled kites, the Dutch Kite to satisfy curiosity: "Is this kite really a bumblebee, flying in spite of itself?" "How will it compare to the workhorse Eddy and Sled?" We scaled sleds up to six feet and down to six inches. Teams were formed to measure the wind, calculate altitude, and record kite weight and area. I encourage kitemakers to keep records. There are many variables in kiteflying and this is the only way to build up comparative data to help in evaluating fresh ideas.

Writing

How to how-to: Get something on paper as you make the first kite: the list of materials and tools and brief notes as you figure out the logical construction sequence. Make several kites to simplify procedures and determine the best sequence. Try to write down each step, no matter how complicated it is to explain. With the diagrams in hand, you can dispense with most of the words, but it clarifies thinking to write it first and rewrite as you go. In the end, good illustrations will take the place of many of the words.

Students in the Anacortes School District who participated in a kite/poetry workshop wrote "kite tales" about imaginary kites, including a pencil kite which "could write across the sky and erase clouds . . . draw on stars and etch on the wind." They made sky signs and imaginary constellations.

How-tos are still another way to write about kites, and can be an introduction to technical writing. I always planned to be a writer when I grew up, but I had no idea of the satisfaction that comes with putting together a lucid, coherent set of instructions.

If someone else is doing the drawings, you may need to make step-by-step mockups for her to work from. Instructions must also have a trial run with a class. Explain what you are doing and invite suggestions. Try to keep it simple. All kites have several options. A beginner meeting all of them at once may be confused.

Sharing the how-to's of kitemaking results in improved designs. The way we first learn to make something can become the "right" way, the "easy" way. Other minds may find shortcuts and improvements. Giving classes allows my students to assist in refining my instructions and methods. The materials commonly used in kitemaking are adapted from other purposes and new kitemakers also bring knowledge of other resources.

Wind Scale

In 1806 Sir Francis Beaufort, an Admiral of the British Navy, devised a wind velocity scale for the use of sailors. Anemometers suitable for use at sea were unavailable, and wind observations and reports were, at best, subjective and imprecise when it came to conveying information on which serious decisions would be based. The Beaufort Scale begins with 0, dead calm, and proceeds to 12, a hurricane. The scale is in nautical miles, equal to about 1.5 miles per hour.

A portion of the scale, adapted for kitefliers, follows. It gives convenient signs for estimating wind conditions and can help foster wind awareness.

1-3	Smoke drifts, scale-like ripples on water
4-7	Leaves rustle, wind felt on face, small wavelets
7-10	Leaves dance, flags ripple, wave crests break
11-16	Blowing dust, small branches move, small waves longer
17-21	Trees sway, kite strings break, moderate waves, some spray
22-27	Large branches move, large waves with foam crests

Flying, Bridles, Lines, Knots, Reels

The first thing to know about flying kites is that the direction of the wind determines the direction in which the kite flies. I am not opposed to running with a kite *per se*, as long as it can be done safely, given the terrain and the available space, but it is not necessary and running in circles, as novice fliers may do, confuses any kite. All the kites in this book fly well in light to moderate (4-15 mph) winds. Many people think of strong winds–20 mph and over–as good kite flying winds, when in fact they can be kite killers. Cell kites do well in fairly high winds, but my own preference is the surprise of learning how slight a breeze it takes to put a well-made kite into the sky.

With a favorable breeze and a little experience, almost all kites can be hand-launched. If ground level wind is not strong enough, try a high launch. With the flier's back to the wind, have a helper take the kite about forty feet downwind. Facing the wind, she holds the kite nose up and releases it at your signal. Pulling in line hand over hand should take the kite into the upper level breezes. High launch is also a good technique for flying sites where ground level winds may be quite squirrelly and turbulent because of buildings and trees.

Sometimes it is best to drop the reel and bring in big "bites" of line by hand, releasing more line as the kite asks for it. Maintain tension as the kite begins to rise. Tugging or pumping on the line also helps to gain altitude. If the wind fails, reeling in and pumping may sustain the kite until the next gust comes along.

Some kites dive on a short line, when you are giving line or reeling in. The remedy when putting a kite up is to start with a helper and quite a bit of line out, so the kite gains altitude in a hurry. If the kite dives when you are bringing it in, run towards it to slacken the line and it will sink to the ground for a soft landing.

In a classroomful of kites, one or two may need tails for stability. If a kite dives or windmills on the end of the line, first check the bridle or tie-on and the kite's symmetry. Tail streamers of plastic or crepe paper are taped or glued to the lower (trailing) edge of the kite. The rule for tails is also symmetry, balanced on both sides. Begin with four-foot lengths and add or subtract. Bowing the kite, as in the Conover Eddy, also helps to stabilize.

If lines tangle and cross, the fliers should walk towards each other. The twist will come down the line and the kites can be separated by exchanging reels or by the fliers walking around each other.

Take your time bringing a kite in. The line comes back on the reel under pressure and can crush it. Wear gloves with strong-pulling kites. If a kite is pulling hard, walk towards it while reeling in to relieve the pressure. Or bring it in hand over hand, paying the line out on the ground. This gives more control. Launching and landing can be dangerous times in the life of a kite. Wind the line after the kite is grounded. In gusty winds, wind in on the slack and wait during the gusts.

Always look the flying site over before taking a class out to fly. Never fly near power lines or highways. Never fly during storms.

Bridles

The starting place for setting the bridle on light kites is the suspension point on the bridle at which the base of the kite forms a 15 degree angle with the horizontal (see Trashbag Box Kite.)

Bridles may need adjustment for different winds. Adjustment to a higher or lower angle changes the portion of kite surface presented to the wind. A higher angle in a strong wind allows more wind to slip away from the lower surface of the kite. A lower angle gives the wind more to push against. To adjust a bridle, first try holding it by one finger, away from the

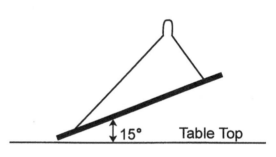

body and into the wind, letting the wind determine the preferred angle. In general, the bridle should be long enough to extend just beyond the wing tips of the kite.

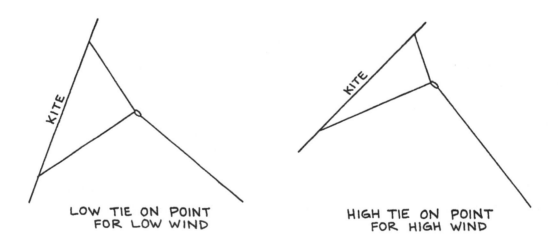

LOW TIE ON POINT
FOR LOW WIND

HIGH TIE ON POINT
FOR HIGH WIND

A ring or small paper clip attached by a larkshead knot or a loop of string over the bridle line allows easy adjustment (see Vietnamese and Square Diamond.) If you are working with a design of your own, or a pattern which does not give complete specifications, a good starting place for flat and bowed kites is to put the towing point approximately one-third of the way down the spine and away from the face of the kite about one-half of the total length of the spine.

Some Kite Terms

Bridle: String which holds the kite into the wind at an angle which makes flight (differentiated from blowing away) possible. **One-point** or **two-point** denotes the number of attachment points. A two-point bridle has two legs. **Bridle legs** are the segments between the kite and the **tow point.** The **flying line** is tied on at the **tow point.**

Keel: Usually made of the same material as the kite and serving the same function as the bridle. Delta kites have keels. They may have several **tow points** for adjustment of the flying angle.

Spars: Bones of the kite. A vertical spar is a **longeron**, or, as in a delta, a **spine.** Cross spars are **horizontals.** In some designs they may be **spreaders,** inserted last to tension the whole structure.

Wing, sail, cover, canopy, skin: The fabric, paper or plastic which cover the kite.

Drag: Resistance to the wind, usually the resistance of the kite line and kite tail.

Reel or winder: Whatever you wrap kite line on.

Kite face: What the observer sees when the kite is flying. The **back** faces the sky. The **leading edges** are the first to meet the wind and the **trailing edges** trail. **Base** is used as in "base of a triangle" to designate the lower edge.

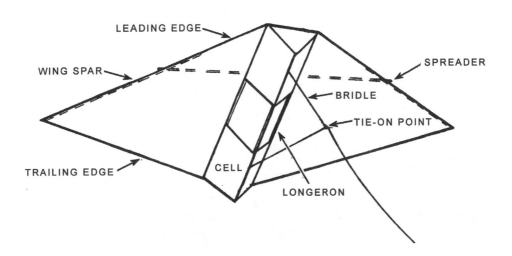

Kite Line

See Classroom Kites for recommendations for the small kites. Commercial cotton "kite twine" is heavy and fuzzy, and inexpensive synthetic kite line frays and ravels. Monofilament fishing line is unpleasant to handle and a hazard on the field since it is nearly invisible. Avoid it.

Braided fishline is a pleasure to use and it is a good idea to have reels with light (under 30#), medium (30#-80#), and heavy (100# or more) to handle various kites in different winds. In light to moderate winds, 30# line will hold most kites but don't risk losing a kite by putting it out past recovery and having a line snap.

Very small (under 12") and miniature kites require fine thread for flying. Look in fabric stores for fine monofilament thread, the exception to the above rule.

Never leave discarded line—or any other trash—on the flying field.

Snap swivels, also used by fishermen, come in several sizes and are wonderful aids to the kiteflier. Tie one on the end of the flying line to eliminate twisting.

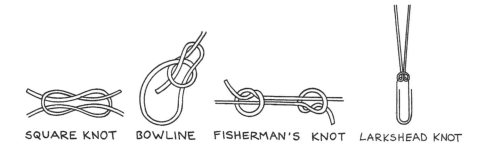

SQUARE KNOT   BOWLINE   FISHERMAN'S KNOT   LARKSHEAD KNOT

Reels and Winders

Reels are a personal decision. Some fliers use any old board or broomstick and others swear by mechanical marvels. If you are a "reel person," a visit to a kite shop will stimulate your imagination. My favorite reels, shown here, are all variations of the notched board. Make them with the grain running the long way. Any child can use them, and this is important to me because I frequently invite bystanders to fly my kites.

Kite shops have various winders for sale, one of the most popular being a plastic ring called a halo, shown on the right.

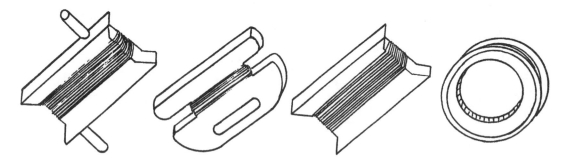

Fabric Kites

My earlier book, *SIMPLE FABRIC KITES*, was written for competent home sewers with little kite experience. The available instructions for cloth kites assumed too much. Many experienced kitemakers also used the book because, while it was not a sewing manual, it gave basic information for kitemakers who did not speak sewing. When you are on speaking terms with your sewing machine and can sew a straight seam, you are ready for fabric kites. As a beginning sewing project, a kite is more interesting than a pillowcase.

The home sewer already understands the essentials of good kitemaking: careful, precise cutting, marking and stitching. Symmetry and precision count. A person who has made a shirt can make a Winged Box or a Flowform. Fitting band to collar, collar to neck, cuffs to sleeves and sleeves to armholes is comparable in difficulty to putting these kites together.

Before you begin, read the introductory material for information on materials sources, fabric choices and kite principles. I have defined some terms as I go along and compiled a brief glossary. I hope this will contribute to a common language because the basic vocabulary of sewing provides a concise means of giving instructions for making fabric kites.

Remember that the Zephyr, Corner and Flowform kites are patented and may not be made to sell.

Fabric

Appropriate fabric is the most important factor. It should be lightweight, non-stretch and non-porous, and these are the criteria by which to judge any fabric. Stability, or freedom from stretch, may be the most important. Kites which lose their shape can't fly well. Flat kites and delta kites can be exceptions to the general rule and will sometimes benefit from a softer hand and limited porosity.

Lightweight sailcloth, also called spinnaker cloth, is the fabric of choice, the material which makes most of these kites possible. Rated at .50 to .75 ounce per yard, it is light in weight, tough and stable. It is a "ripstop" material, meaning that a slightly heavier thread is woven at intervals into both the warp and the weft.

Sailcloth comes in several widths, 40"-41", 54", 60". Sailcloth rated at 1.5 oz is also available, but is not necessary or even desirable for any of the kites in this book.

I do advise beginning kitemakers to start with sailcloth. When considering alternatives, a general rule is that the materials used should be as lightweight as is possible for the winds in which the kite will be flown. Keep the rule in mind and compromise as necessary. The field test for porosity is to hold the fabric to your lips and blow. If your breath comes through, so will the wind which is supposed to lift the kite.

A new kitemaker may assume that ripstop is ripstop and that the outdoor-wear fabric in the fabric shop is what is called for. Not so, chiefly because of the stretch factor. Tug on the bias and see how the fabric moves out of shape. Kite shops and mail order suppliers listed in the Resource List have spinnaker sailcloth.

The kites in this section range from very easy to pay-attention-and-follow-the-instructions complexity. As the designs become more complex, the options, the possible ways to do things, increase in number. Some of the instructions suggest alternative solutions.

Sewing Aids

♦   Good **scissors** and a **seam ripper** are essential.

♦   **Dressmakers' tracing paper** and **tracing wheel**: Large sheets of carbon-type paper in light and dark colors. A fast way to transfer pattern markings to fabric. Mark two pieces at once, and identically, by sandwiching two layers of fabric, wrong sides together, between two sheets of tracing paper, carbon against the fabric.

♦   **Tailor's chalk, dressmaker's marking pencils** and ordinary colored pencils can be used for marking. If construction marks don't matter on the finished kite, use pencil.

♦   A **straight edge** facilitates marking. A **framing square** aids pattern drafting.

♦   If edges will be finished by hemming instead of hot cutting, consider the **rotary wheel cutter** and **mat** which quilters use. Several layers of fabric can be stacked and cut together. Quilters' 6"-wide plastic rulers are handy for aligning edges.

♦   I use pieces of **quarry tile** to hold layers of fabric and patterns in place. **Dressmakers' weights** serve the same purpose. So do runners' ankle and wrist weights, coffee mugs, silverware or cans of soup.

♦   Use **Fray Check** to do just that. Run a bead along a trailing edge and it can even substitute for hot-cutting.

- **Masking tape** or **gluestick** for fabric will hold fabric pieces in place for stitching. Use lightly outside the stitching line because they will gum the needle. **Washaway Wonder Tape**, available in some fabric stores, is a one-fourth inch wide doublestick tape which is very easy to apply and can be stitched through.

  DryLine permanent adhesive, found in office supply stores, is useful for seams. Just draw a bead of adhesive along one of the edges. Minimum gumming of needle.

- **3M ReMount** repositionable adhesive is excellent for applique and fabric overlay. May be sewed through. The needle will have to be cleaned occasionally. Use only in a well-ventilated area.

- Other useful items: **grommets** and small **eyelets** for reinforcing holes. **Polyester grosgrain ribbon** or **twill tape** is good for binding, sleeves, loops, pockets and reinforcements. Seal cut ends with a hot knife or a flame. Kite and outdoor wear stores may have still other tapes and webbings. **Adhesive-backed fabric,** sold for mending and decorating, is handy for mending and for reinforcing stress points. After it is applied, pressing with a barely warm iron improves adhesion. Test on scraps first.

Tape can also be made by hot cutting a 1 1/4"-wide strip on the straight of the material. Fold and press before applying with straight or zigzag stitch. Piece binding on the bias as shown to avoid seam bulk. If you have a binder attachment for your sewing machine learn to use it.

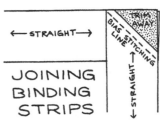

- **Shoelaces** make good drawstrings for kite bags.

- Supplies from the fishing counter include **split rings, snap swivels** and **plastic tubing**. The hardware store has **plastic tubing** and **dowels**. Plastic tubing may be used for joining spars and for spreader connections. It comes in many sizes. Take a scrap of dowel to the hardware store and test for an inner diameter which gives a snug fit.

- The kites in this book can all be sparred with dowels, light in weight, readily available, easy to replace. **Fiberglass** and **graphite** rods are available from shops which sell kitemaking materials. **Plastic end caps** keep rods from poking through fabric.

Cutting, General

When cutting with scissors, use the method described for slicing through plastic with the blades barely opened. Observe the clerk at the fabric counter. Straight edges may be cut with a knife or a roller cutter.

Hot-Cutting Synthetic Fabric

♦   The **hot knife** used by kitemakers is essentially a soldering iron with a chisel tip. You may already have a tool which will work. My first hot knife was a woodburning iron. If you are shopping, look for a 500-degree minimum temperature. A good iron should move through the fabric without dragging, beading the edge, or giving off fumes. Keep the tip clean with steel wool or by lightly filing it. A soldering iron or woodburner may come with a selection of tips. A pencil tip is good for tacking, a chisel tip for cutting.

♦   **Hot-cutting** may produce fumes from the melted fabric. Some people are sensitive to these and, in any case, they are not good to breathe. Always ventilate the work area.

♦   The pencil tip **hot tacker** is used to baste sailcloth pieces together before stitching or when adding trim and reinforcements. Work against a straight edge.

♦   **Glass** is the preferred cutting surface, far and away the best. Formica and Masonite will work. Some metal straight edges draw too much of the heat away from the knife. My aluminum yardstick works well. My steel carpenter's square does not. Try what you have to find what works.

♦   **Formica, Masonite and sheet metal make good patterns** for frequent use. Paper works for one-time use and tagboard (like file folders) for several times. If you can find it, oil board, used for stencils, is superior. These three have the advantage of being inexpensive and easily cut with scissors. I use tagboard for most of my patterns, making new ones when the edges are no longer true. If a pattern sticks to the melted edge, separate it from the fabric carefully with a narrow blade such as a letter opener.

♦   **Patterns** made from heavier material hold the fabric firmly in place while you are cutting. Weights around the edges do the same. For fine detail, as for applique, I hold the pattern down with the eraser end of a pencil. Move the knife fast enough for a clean cut.

♦   **Bill Goble's system of pre-assembly** by hot-tacking pieces together, followed by trimming with a hot knife to bond the edges, is the easiest way to handle sailcloth, particularly when joining long pieces. Allow one-fourth inch for trim and one-fourth inch for the seam. Line up the edges to be joined. Align your metal straight edge close to the edges. Hot tack the edges together with a hot tacker or by nicking the edges at intervals with the chisel tip. Place the straight edge one-fourth inch from the tacked outer edges and trim, thus bonding the pieces together before stitching.

Some Sewing Terms

Selvage: The woven, non-raveling edges of a piece of fabric.

Grain: The direction of the threads in woven fabric. "Straight grain" or "with the grain" means in the direction of the weave.

Off-grain: Across the threads of the weave. **Bias** is diagonally across the weave.

Right side/wrong side: On prints, the printed side is the right side. Some weaves, including most sailcloth, do not have a clearly-evident right or wrong side. The coated side is "right" in coated material.

Narrow hem: Turn 1/4" by pressing or creasing. Turn again 1/4" and stitch near the folded edge.

Backstitch: Take half a dozen stitches back along a seam in order to secure the ends of the stitching. Or set the stitch length at zero and take several stitches in place for the same purpose.

Edgestitch: Stitch close to the free edge of the material, as for a hem or sleeve.

Some Sewing Tips

♦ **Mark** the right side of the fabric and the top or leading edge of each piece with chalk. Assembly is easier if you know which way is up.

♦ **Plan** the steps for efficiency. First, cut and mark. If the design calls for pressing, do it all at once. Finally, stitch. Plan ahead to reinforce the ends of sleeves and the bridle attachment points with extra fabric or fabric tape. Apply the reinforcements before closing the sleeves. Reinforce eyelet and grommet sites. Reinforcements are important. One crash can poke a spar through a single layer fabric sleeve. Reinforcing after the fact is much more difficult.

♦ **Sewing machines** commonly have both narrow and wide presser feet. The narrow foot may be the best choice for stitching 1/4" seams. Familiarize yourself with other attachments, particularly zipper, hemming and binding feet. The zipper foot facilitates close-in stitching, for example, closing a sleeve after spar insertion. When you face miles of tail streamers, the hemmer is the answer. Practice on scraps.

- **Match needle size to fabric weight,** just as you would with conventional fabrics. I like a size 11 or size 14 needle (sharp, not ballpoint) for spinnaker sailcloth. Sailcloth dulls needles. Change when needed, you can hear a dull needle thump when it hits the fabric. Use eight to ten stitches to the inch. Backstitch all seams. Use a heavier needle when stitching webbing or several thicknesses of cloth.

- **Guiterman polyester thread** is what I use. Ordinary cotton-covered polyester is fine for small-to medium-size kites. Buy standard brands. Five-for-one-dollar bargains are worth what you pay.

- **Sailcloth's** high strength, light weight and stability make it ideal for kites. The coating which, for the kitemaker's purposes, adds body and stability, also makes it slippery. Some special handling may be necessary to get it through the machine in good style. To control sailcloth while stitching, consider a Teflon foot, which is an ordinary presser foot with a Teflon layer on the bottom. I use it for all my sewing. A "walking foot" is more expensive, but can be the solution to the unequal feed which is common with two layers of slick material. Tissue paper, placed between the fabric and the feed dogs, can be torn away after stitching.

- **Put the off-grain edge on top** to minimize stretch when you join an off-grain edge to an on-grain edge. Dressmakers sew from "wide to narrow," stitching with the grain of the fabric rather than against it. Following this principle on delta kites, you would stitch the sleeves on the leading edges from the base to the top. To enhance symmetry on any kite, stitch matching seams and hems in the same direction, generally top to bottom. Examples: delta and sled spar and spine sleeves and sled fins.

- **Zigzag seams** or their variations with several stitches on each zig have more give than straight seams. Some Facet Kite makers use a long stitch with a very narrow zigzag for joining squares.

- **Calculate yardage** from the dimensions given in the pattern. Because kites are often pieced in multi-colors, yardage is not always specified. A **proportional scale,** commonly known as a **proportion wheel,** is a handy, inexpensive, easy-to-use tool for scaling kite patterns to larger and smaller sizes. It is found in graphic arts and office supply stores.

- A **framing string** made of braided kite line or button thread may be enclosed in hems to control stretch.

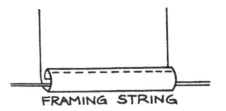

FRAMING STRING

Pressing

If possible, store your stock of sailcloth rolled on a tube. If it *must* be pressed use a dry iron on a low setting. Start very low and practice on scraps. Too much heat can curl coated material like a dead leaf. Protect the fabric by covering it with a dry press cloth or a sheet of tissue paper. My iron has a Teflon sole plate, which is ideal, but not so necessary that you should buy a new iron in order to make kites. Sleeves and hems can be creased or finger pressed instead of ironed.

When you join two pieces of material do not press the seam open because the stitches then become the weakest link. Press the seam to one side and stitch the edges down about one-fourth inch from the seam.

Dressmakers' Knot

Robin Dennell, writing in *Natural History* magazine, says that "the sewing needle is probably the most underrated invention in the entire upper paleolithic." The needle is said to have made its debut some 23,000 years ago in southwestern France. The headline for the article on paleolithic tools reads "Sewing is probably *Homo sapiens'* most underrated technological advance."

Perhaps the most underrated knot is the end-of-the-line knot used in hand sewing. You can use it on bridle ends for plastic kites to insure that they won't slip out of the tape. It is useful at the end of any line to keep knots or loops from slipping. I always lick my forefinger before I wrap the thread around it. Something my mother taught me.

ROLL THE THREADS TOGETHER BETWEEN THUMB AND FINGER

PULL ROLLED THREADS INTO KNOT

Kite Directory

I have rated the kites on a 1-4 scale, ranging from very easy to difficult. Several factors enter into this assessment. A three-legged bridle, for example, is difficult enough to put a simple kite like the Whole Bag Kite in the 2 instead of the 1 category.

The directory will be useful chiefly to teachers and others planning kitemaking for particular skill levels. No one should be put off by a "somewhat difficult" rating. Care and precision will pay off with flying kites.

Almost all of these kites can be made of paper, plastic, or fabric. As kitemakers gain experience, they will recognize other options and variations. Skim through the book for ideas. Many of the construction details which are given for individual kites can be adapted to other kite designs.

1. Very Easy

paper: Vietnamese Kite
Stapled Sled Kite
Bookmark Sled Kite
Conover Eddy Kite
Lee Toy's Eddy Kite

plastic: Vietnamese Bag Kite
Trashbag Sled Kite
Mini-Sled Kite
Conover Eddy Kite
Lee Toy's Eddy Kite

2. Easy

paper: Siamese Snake Kite
Bag Snake Kite

plastic: Plastic Snake Kite
Mini Bullet Kite
Plastic Bullet Kite
Whole Bag Kite
Fantasmo Kite

fabric: Fabric Square Kite
Square Diamond Kite

3. Somewhat Difficult

paper: Dutch Kite
Paper Dragon Kite
Traditional Eddy Kite

plastic: Little Delta Kite
One-Piece Delta Kite
Tony Cyphert Delta Kite
Joseph Lee Delta Bird Kite
Trashbag Box Kite
Mini Winged Box Kite

fabric: Fabric Snake Kite
Hornbeam Sled Kite
Harper's Ferry Delta Kite
Zephyr Delta Kite
French Military Kite
Winged Square Box Kite
One-cell Corner Kite

4. Difficult

fabric: Two-cell Corner Kite
Four-sided Facet Kite
Five-sided Facet Kite
Flow Form Kite

KITES

TO MAKE

Vietnamese Kite

In 1976, in a Bicentennial crafts program in our local schools, I was teaching sixth grade students to make the Siamese Snake Kite, when a boy recently arrived from Vietnam came up holding a piece of the bamboo reed and saying, "Can I show you the kite we make in Vietnam?" It provides a simple introduction to the kites of the Orient and is one of my favorite classroom kites. Made with the newspaper which covered the work table, this little kite has proved to be a jewel.

Dimensions are given in the layout, as they must be if someone who has not seen the kite is to build it, but when I teach the Vietnamese Kite in the classroom we eyeball it. Some kites will be fat, a few will be skinny, and one or two may be bridled upside-down, but all will fly. There can hardly be a better introduction to kitemaking. There is a pleasing symmetry in having a kite which has delighted Asian children for thousands of years brought to our schools by a new immigrant in our Bicentennial year.

Newspaper and tissue paper are both light enough for a small kite. Crepe paper tails add stability and movement. They may be placed according to the character of the kite (fish or fowl.) Begin with four strips of crepe paper, approximately 1"x5'. The dimensions of the bamboo spars vary, because individual kitemakers use different proportions for the folds. They are approximately 14 1/2" for the spine and 22" for the arched cross spar. I break the reeds to the desired length.

Vietnamese Kite Instructions

Materials: 12" square of tissue or newspaper, plus scraps
1" wide crepe paper streamers for tails
matchstick bamboo reed
26" string for bridle
gluestick

Tools: scissors, pencil, ruler

1. Wrong side of paper up, crease on dotted lines.
2. Measure spine and glue in place as shown.
3. Measure the reed for the cross spar. Choose a strong reed with a symmetrical curve. It should arch close to the leading edges.
4. Glue the corner flaps over the reed. Glue one side first, without trying to hold the curve in place; then glue the other side. (Extra hands can help here and kitemakers may want to work in pairs for this step.) Glue reinforcements over the reed intersection and between the center and the corners as shown.

5. **TURN KITE OVER** and bridle. Glue on tails.

easy to make
easy to fly
light/medium winds

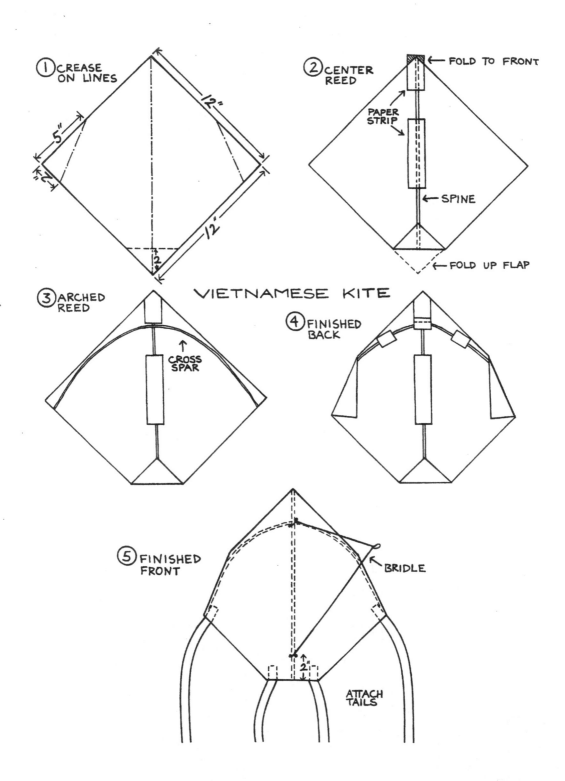

① CREASE ON LINES

12"
5"
2"
12"
12"
2"

② CENTER REED
← FOLD TO FRONT
PAPER STRIP
SPINE
← FOLD UP FLAP

VIETNAMESE KITE

③ ARCHED REED
CROSS SPAR

④ FINISHED BACK

⑤ FINISHED FRONT
BRIDLE
2"
ATTACH TAILS

Vietnamese Bag Kite

The Vietnamese Kite can also be made from a high-density polyethylene bag, with the lower part of the bag fringed. The bag should be slightly taller than it is wide. One bag will make two kites. Smaller sizes will work but 16" is large enough to fly well and small enough to be framed with bamboo reed. Trim the sealed bottom edge off. Spread the bag out and flatten the gussets, if any, and slit up the sides.

Fold the bag as shown. Mark the lower edge. Unfold and trim away at the top. Cut the fringe. Now, consult the instructions for the Vietnamese paper kite. The spars are taped instead of glued in place. Bridle as for the paper Vietnamese.

easy to make
easy to fly
light/medium winds

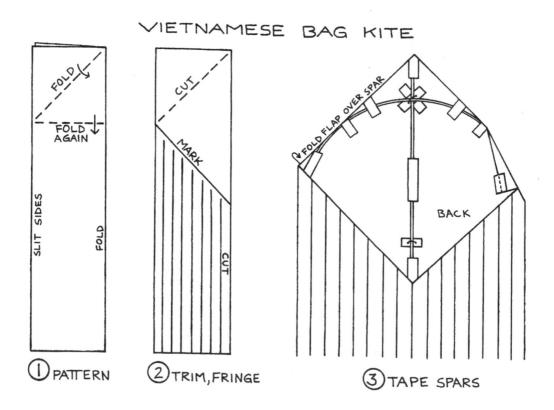

VIETNAMESE BAG KITE

① PATTERN ② TRIM, FRINGE ③ TAPE SPARS

Siamese Snake Kite

Snake, sometimes called Cobra or Dragon, kites are now commonplace. They are made of various materials, with tails 100 feet and more in length, and can be purchased at most toy counters. It was over thirty years ago at the Seattle World's Fair that I saw my first Snake, hanging on the wall in the Thailand shop. The face, a cobra with a gaping mouth, was painted on white tissue. The 12' long tail was green crepe paper with painted black scales, tapering to a tip of red tissue. Though fabric or mylar snake kites are beautiful, my own favorite is still tissue and crepe paper.

When I bring Snake Kites to a classroom and someone asks, "Will that kite fly?" I reply, "It would be silly for me to go around the schools teaching people to make kites that won't fly." But the Snake design was a great departure from my early limited experience with kites and, when I first saw it, I asked the clerk, "Will it fly?" She said, "Oh, yes, it flies very high." I supposed that to be a reply given to sell kites, but I bought one and put it away until Spring. When I finally flew it, I was so excited by its appearance and action in the sky that I brought it home, laid it on the table and dissected it to learn how it was made.

The Siamese Snake, then, was the first of the Classroom Kites. It is easy to handle but children think of it as big and powerful.

Matchstick bamboo reed is the framing material for the Snake. The longest reed needed for this kite is 26". When preparing for a class, separate a number of reeds from the blind. Some will be too flimsy to bend into a strong, symmetrical arch and should be reserved for use as reinforcements in other kites.

My first Snake had a 12' tail. When I first began teaching this kite a roll of crepe paper was ten feet long. Now it is 7 1/2', and this is the length that we use for classroom Snakes. No two tails need be alike. Because framing the face is a four-hand job, this kite requires teamwork. If each member of the team selects a different color, and the crepe paper is cut in 1'-2' strips, the tail can be pieced with alternating colors.

Wrap the tail around the kite face for storage.

Make patterns for a class by cutting several at once from a stack of newspaper.

Siamese Snake Kite

Materials: tissue paper, 11"x15", plus scraps
crepe paper, 5"x7 1/2', cut across grain
matchstick bamboo reed
lightweight string, 60", for bridle
gluestick

Tools: scissors, pencil, ruler, paper cutter

1. Lay the pattern on the tissue and draw around it. Cut out.

2. Measure the reed by bending around the curved edge, about 1/2" in from the edge of the paper and ending about 1 1/2" from the bottom (straight) edge on each side. Break off the correct length.

3. Spread glue on the outer 1" of the curved edge only. One person holding the reed tips in place while another folds the glued tissue over the reed will keep the kite face flat.

    Find the center of the kite and mark a vertical line down the middle. Measure a reed for the spine which runs from the top of the arch to 1½" from the base. Cover with tissue. Cut two reeds to fit between the ends of the arch. Cover with a tissue strip.

4. **TURN KITE OVER.** This is the front or face of the kite. Bridle as shown with the ends of the string going down from the front, up from the back and tied over the reed. Holes may be poked with the pencil tip.

5. Glue on the tail.

    If this is a Flying Day, hold the bridle string over one finger, and when the wind lifts the kite to a good flying angle, tie a loop at that point. Flying line is tied through the loop. In a very light breeze, the tail may be shortened. (See Bridles for more information on the correct bridle angle for a light kite.)

fairly easy to make
easy to fly
light/medium winds

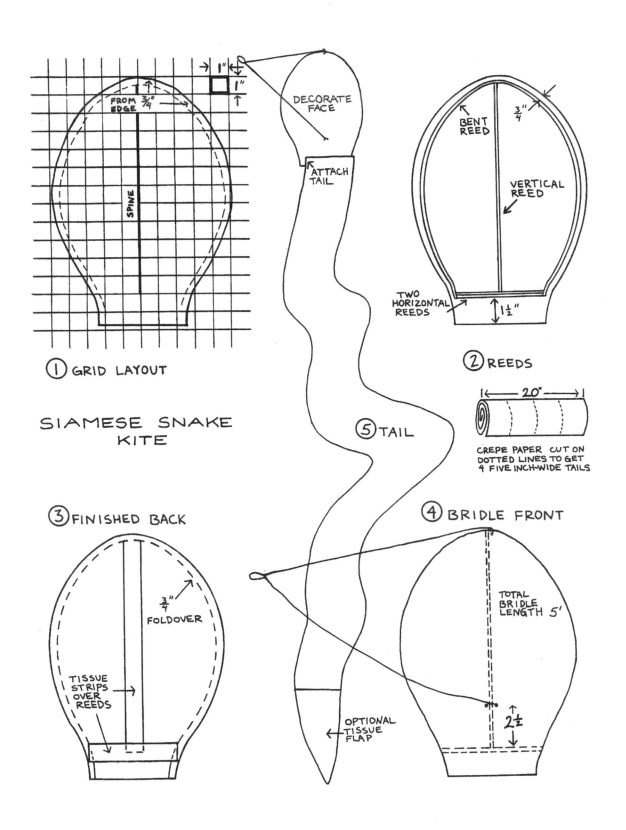

① GRID LAYOUT

SIAMESE SNAKE KITE

1"
1"
FROM EDGE 3/4
SPINE

DECORATE FACE
ATTACH TAIL

② REEDS

BENT REED
3/4
VERTICAL REED
TWO HORIZONTAL REEDS
1½"

20"
CREPE PAPER CUT ON DOTTED LINES TO GET 4 FIVE INCH-WIDE TAILS

③ FINISHED BACK

3/4
FOLDOVER
TISSUE STRIPS OVER REEDS

⑤ TAIL

OPTIONAL TISSUE FLAP

④ BRIDLE FRONT

TOTAL BRIDLE LENGTH 5'
2½

Bag Snake Kite

This low-cost version of the Snake came from Gary Hinze of San Jose. The brown grocery bag and the newspaper tail are dramatic in the sky, with a dark and somewhat ominous appearance. The kite tail must be softened by crumpling and smoothing out several times. Otherwise, it is too stiff for stability. When I demonstrate this kite, it always surprises the class to see me suddenly crumple and crush the kite tail which I have so carefully assembled.

Materials: large grocery bag with end removed and one edge slit open
(makes two kite faces)
1/8" dowels, 16" and 12" long
cellophane tape
gluestick
newspaper for tail
lightweight string, 60", for bridle

Tools: cardboard template, scissors, ruler, pencil, paper cutter

1-2. Mark the bridle points and the end points for the spars on the bag after tracing the pattern. Cut out.

3. Tape as shown, cross spar first.

4. Bridle as shown.

5. Tail strips may be cut on the paper cutter, a whole section of newspaper at once.

    Octopus tail: four strips, approximately 8"x28", glued end to end, and cut in 2" strips as shown. Glue top edge to back of kite.

    Snake tail: ten strips, glued end to end and tapered.

IMPORTANT: To soften the newspaper, crumple and smooth out the finished Snake tail at least three times. Otherwise, the tail wags the kite. The tail may be shortened for light winds.

medium difficulty
easy to fly
light/medium winds

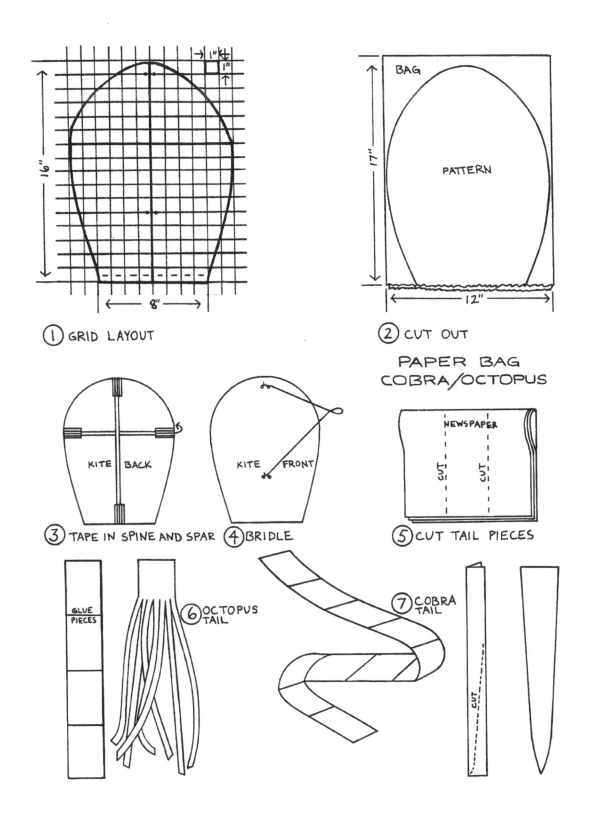

① GRID LAYOUT

② CUT OUT

PAPER BAG
COBRA/OCTOPUS

③ TAPE IN SPINE AND SPAR ④ BRIDLE

⑤ CUT TAIL PIECES

⑥ OCTOPUS TAIL

⑦ COBRA TAIL

Plastic Snake Kite

Here is another Snake, a variation by Joan Newcomb, dressed in plastic and constructed by working over a pattern (See the Joseph Lee Delta Kite for this procedure.) Draw the kite outline on paper, marking the location of the center spar. Tape this pattern to the work surface and spread the plastic over the pattern, taping it down.

Materials: sheet plastic, 1 mil or less and about 9"x12", plus 5" wide tail strips
matchstick bamboo reed
cellophane tape, 1/2" wide
lightweight string for bridle, 60"

Tools: paper for pattern, scissors, marking pen

1. Curve the reed around the kite face and cut or break it to size. Tape in place, first tacking the tips and the center with 2"-3" lengths of tape. Cover the spine and the reeds at the base with tape. Cut out the kite by running the scissors along the outer edge of the tape.

    The tail, 5" wide by about 10' long, may be made of plastic scraps. Tape to the lower edge of the kite. If the tail twists in flight, tape reed battens across the width at 2' intervals.

2. **TURN KITE OVER** and bridle as shown in the instructions for the Siamese Snake.

fairly easy to make
easy to fly
light/medium winds

PLASTIC SIAMESE SNAKE

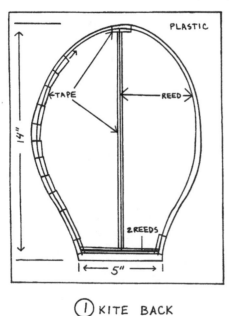

① KITE BACK

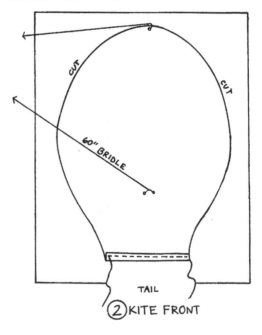

② KITE FRONT

Fabric Snake Tail

The tail should be 20'-30' long and as wide as the base of the finished kite plus one-half inch hem allowance on each side. Hemming gives the tail more body and minimizes twisting. The top edge of the tail should be on the straight of the material. See Tails for more ideas.

Only the last ten feet or so of the tail need to be tapered. Join the sections with lapped seams to form sleeves for the battens. Battens are 1/8" dowels used for stiffening at the base of the kite and at intervals on the tail to minimize twisting. If the tail is one-piece, tape sleeves can be sewed on at 3' intervals.

Hem the edges and cut a small hole in each sleeve to insert the batten.

Attach the tail to the kite with a lapped seam and insert a batten 3" shorter than the base of the kite.

Several variables determine the optimum length of the tail, material weight being one. Keep it light. The kite face should be of non-porous fabric, generally sailcloth, but the tail can be sheer, with printed voile and nylon organdy as examples. The tail can also be made of sailcloth.

If the wind is strong, and the kite dives or pinwheels, more tail is needed. (Check the bridle angle, too.) The Fabric Snake is rugged and can fly in winds much too strong for its classic paper counterpart. Even in light winds, it can carry a lot of tail. If it is struggling to rise in a light breeze, it may be necessary to shorten the tail. Adding the end section with a strip of Velcro, which also serves as a batten, makes this easy.

OTHER
SNAKE DESIGNS

Fabric Snake Kite (27' tail)

Materials: One and one-half yards of 40" wide material are needed if kite and tail are made of the same material. More likely, you will want contrasting kite face and tail. The tail may be pieced of several colors. The kite face may be decorated by piecing or applique. This should be done after cutting out and before construction. Self-adhesive material is handy for reinforcements. Polyester twill tape ends may be sealed by hot cutting or passing through a candle or lighter flame.

> 1/8"-3/16" fiberglass rod, 4' long
> 3/16" dowel for spine and cross spar
> 1/8" dowel scraps for tail battens, if needed
> 5/8" wide polyester twill tape for sleeves
> 5' of 30# test line for bridle

1. Reinforce the ends of sleeves and the bridle points with 1 1/2" squares of material.

2. Stitch on the seam line around the curved edge of kite. Turn and press towards the wrong side on the seam line. Stitch close to the edge to form the sleeve, backstitching at beginning and end. Leave both ends open.

3. To form the horizontal sleeve, center 5/8" wide tape on the sleeve line from the edge of the outer sleeve on the left side across the kite face to the corresponding right edge, turning the raw ends under. Beginning at the left, backstitch and edgestitch up the long side, across the end, and down the other side, ending with backstitching, and leaving the end open to insert the spar.

4. Stitch the sleeve for the spine in the same way, breaking the stitching at the horizontal sleeve and leaving the lower end open.

5. Both the outside framing spar and the spine should end three-fourths inch from the base, leaving a flap for attaching the tail. Tape the tips of the fiberglass or use plastic end caps. Carefully work the fiberglass spar into the sleeve, trimming it to size. Insert the dowels. Close the sleeves.

6. Bridle the Snake, using a needle and thread. Tie the bridle over the spars.

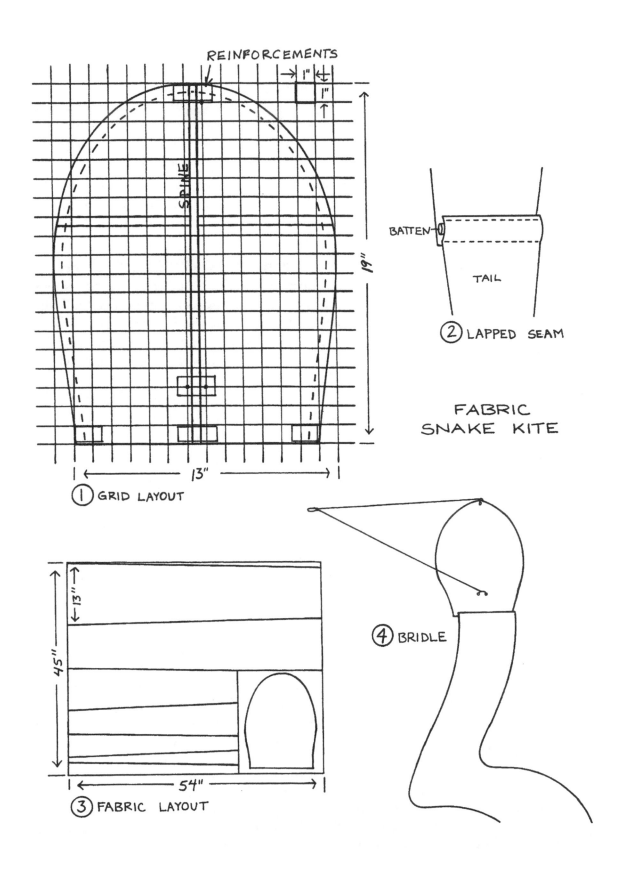

REINFORCEMENTS

SPINE

19"

13"

① GRID LAYOUT

BATTEN

TAIL

② LAPPED SEAM

FABRIC
SNAKE KITE

13"

45"

54"

③ FABRIC LAYOUT

④ BRIDLE

Paper Kites

Dutch Kite

This all-paper kite is adapted from a design by A. van Breda. Make it of butcher paper, which schools have in 36"-wide rolls in bright colors and which may be available in 12"-wide rolls from paper supply stores. The latter comes in dispenser boxes and is labeled "craft paper". Grocery bags and medium weight brown kraft paper are other possibilities. Pin the Dutch Kite to a corkboard to store it.

When I first show the Dutch Kite in the classroom, people nudge each other and whisper, "It'll never fly, Wilbur!" But I have my moment when I demonstrate that it flies well, is remarkably durable, and might be made on the spur of the moment of materials found around the house.

The design of the Dutch Kite puts it in the "two-stick, flat kite" category. It is such a singularly successful kite, so durable and versatile, that every kitemaker should have a Dutch Kite up her sleeve. It incorporates the basic elements needed for flight– a spine, a crosspiece, a bridle to hold the kite face to the wind, and a tail for stability. It flies easily in light and medium winds, can be towed by a bicycle rider or walked around the park by a three-year-old. It is tolerant; the less-than-perfect kite will fly.

Making a Dutch Kite calls upon many skills–measuring, folding, cutting, gluing and tying. Lee Wilbur of Kennewick, who used the Dutch Kite in his first grade classes, added matchstick bamboo reed reinforcements in the spine and cross spar to make it more rugged.

Dutch Kites fly well in train, the kind of kite train which is called a tree, with branches going off the main line at intervals. Use 15# test line for the master line, and let the first kite out about 50 feet. Using crochet thread or other light flying line, put a second kite up about 25 feet. Tie a loop in the master line. Break off the second line from the spool and tie it through the loop. You now have two kites on one line, and can continue adding other kites in the same manner. Bringing a train in can be difficult. An extra pair of hands and a box to stack them in helps avoid tangles.

Small and Miniature Dutch Kites

A miniature Dutch Kite has won in the "smallest kite" category in several kite festivals. The standard Dutch Kite begins with a 12"x16" sheet of paper, a ratio of three to four. Kites scaled larger than this are giraffes, subject to slipped discs and other back ailments, but the design works well in smaller sizes, down to 3" x 4" before folding. Use crisp, lightweight paper such as onion skin and broom straw for the bridle stays. Make the folds and the scraps for the bridle assembly as narrow as possible. Skinny strips of crepe paper or the mylar strips which come in a pack for gift wrapping will make the tail. Fly on "Crystal" thread, a fine monofilament sold in sewing centers. Anything heavier would mean a flying line which weighs more than the kite. These pocket-sized kites fly well, but they need a fairly strong wind and considerable skill, since surface winds are turbulent.

Paper Dragon Kite

The Paper Dragon Kite is another design by A. van Breda. I talk to myself as I work with it. Is it a good idea to include it as a classroom kite? It is relatively difficult, somewhat fragile, must be hung to store, and cannot take strong winds. But laying out the grid is an elegant measuring exercise, and as cell kites go, the construction is simple. A flying Paper Dragon is breathtaking, well worth the effort. I have used it in junior high and middle school classes.

Made of butcher paper, and reinforced with dowel, this design is well suited to playful decoration, with toenails, eyes, teeth and vertical or horizontal stripes as possibilities. Colored marking pens on white butcher paper will give a translucent effect. Glued-on scraps of foil wrapping paper are particularly fine. The extended flaps on both sides (toenails) may be fringed and then curled by drawing them over the blade of the scissors.

The Paper Dragon requires more class time than some of the other kites, at least two periods to allow for imaginative decoration. There are two ways to approach this kite in class. One way is to prepare a sample set of "stages" in dragon development.

Stage 1. Full-size drawing of the basic horizontal and vertical grid. The accompanying handout should give dimensions, so students can copy the grid.
Stage 2. Cut out kite, with folds creased.
Stage 3. Completed kite, including the bridle.

If the samples are posted and a handout with the sequence of steps is available, students who have some experience with the simpler kites should be able to proceed on their own.

Another way is to provide kite paper ready-cut to size and stencils with cuts for the legs, eyes and corners, ready to trace on the kite paper. Vertical fold lines can then be drawn and the proper cuts made. Samples of the cut out, folded and finished kite should be available so that how to move from a flat sheet of paper to a flying winged prism is clear.

Box or cell kites are heavier than single-plane kites. The Paper Dragon needs a medium wind. A skyful of multi-colored Dragons costumed as fish, crayfish, caterpillars, praying mantises or other insects is a fine sight.

The Dragon needs several 5'- 6' tail streamers. It can be scaled to 24"x12", and I have made and flown a mini-dragon, beginning with 12"x8" paper. I pin the Dragon to a corkboard for storage.

Dutch Kite

Materials: stiff paper (butcher), 12"x16"
paper scraps for bridle assembly
light string, 26"
matchstick bamboo reed for reinforcement
crepe paper for tail 1"x4'
gluestick

Tools: pencil, scissors, ruler, paper cutter

1-2. Fold and crease the paper the long way. Fold and crease again 3/4" from the center fold. Open flat so the folded section forms a vertical ridge up the middle (spine). This is the front of the kite.

3-4. Open the paper flat, ridge side down. Fold and crease on a line 3" from the top (short way). Fold and crease 3/4" from this fold. This forms the cross spar. Cut as shown on the solid dark lines in Dia. 4.

5-6. Open the paper flat. Brush glue between the fold lines on top and bottom sections of the long vertical fold but not on the cross section with the slit. Lay bamboo reed, cut to size, on the center crease, a short length above the cross fold, and a long piece below. Fold and crease, thus gluing the spine.

6-7. The cut flaps at the intersection of vertical and cross spar folds should slide over each other, one coming out on the front of the kite, the other on the back. Glue these flaps down.

7-8. On the back, brush glue on the cross spar area. Lay bamboo reed in the crease and fold to form the cross spar. Trim the top corners of the kite.

Making the Bridle

Take two scraps of paper, each 2"x2 1/2", and fold in half, across the 2" dimension. Fold in half the other way and snip a small corner off the center fold, making a hole in the center of the paper. On one scrap, cut about 3/4" up the middle fold.

Open the scrap up. Tie a 2" length of bamboo reed to each end of the 26" string. Thread the sticks through the holes in the scraps so they ride in the creases and the papers are linked by the string.

Glue the scrap with the slit over the intersection of the spars, parallel to the spine. The other scrap is glued over the spine at the base of the kite.

Consult Bridling to set the Dutch Kite bridle.

Glue on tail. Add more if the wind is strong and the kite flies erratically. If the wind is very light and the kite will not rise, trim the tail.

fairly easy to make
easy to fly
light/medium winds

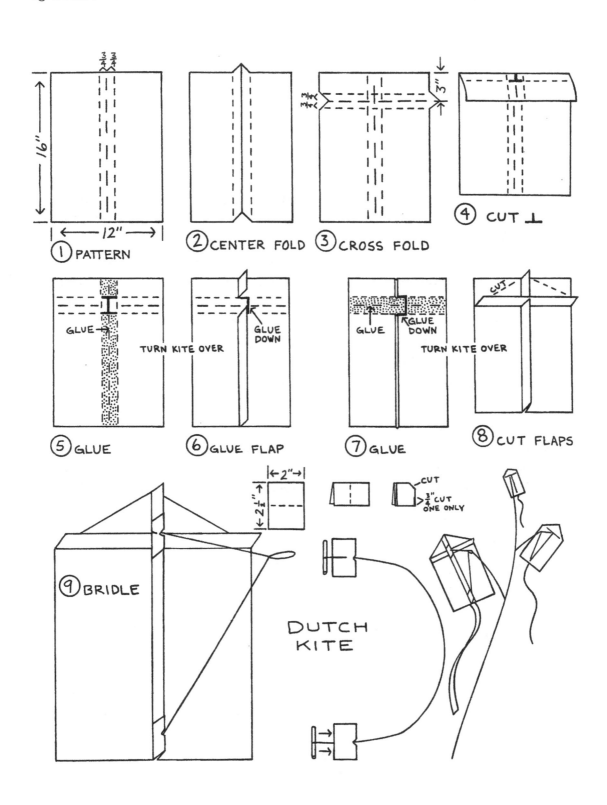

Paper Dragon Kite

Materials: butcher paper, 12"x36"
1/8" dowel, 26" long
cellophane tape
lightweight string, 36"
1" wide crepe paper for tails
gluestick

Tools: yardstick, ruler, pencil, scissors or Exacto knife, needle

1.   Draw cutting and folding lines on paper.

2.   Cut on solid lines as shown. Decorating may be done now, since stripes or other designs in the cell interior are easier to work out before the folds are made.

3.   Fold and crease on the dotted lines. To visualize where the glue goes, that is, on the inner edge of one flap and the outer edge of the other, pull the prism together to see how the flaps fit on top of each other to form the spine. Brush glue on the flaps. Place the dowel in the fold before the flaps are brought together to form the reinforced leading edge.

Reinforce the bridle points with tape and bridle as shown, poking holes through the paper, and tying the string over the reinforcing dowel. See Bridling for setting the angle. Glue on tails.

4.   You might want to add butcher paper wings to the Dragon, as shown in the drawing. The wings are designed by laying the completed Dragon on a sheet of paper and sketching a pleasing shape. Fold the paper, cutting the two identical wings together. Reinforce with a dowel across the top edge from one wingtip to the other. After the Dragon body is firmly glued to the wings, a vertical spar from the top of the kite to the base of the wings is added to the back (dotted lines). Tape or glue it to the outside. The Winged Dragon flies well.

somewhat difficult to make
easy to fly
medium wind

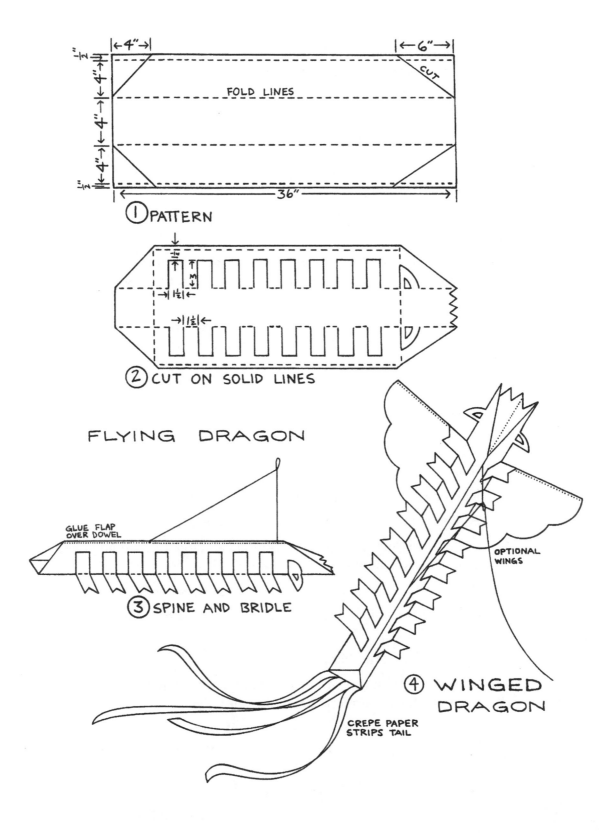

① PATTERN

② CUT ON SOLID LINES

FLYING DRAGON

③ SPINE AND BRIDLE

④ WINGED DRAGON

Sled Kites

William Allison patented his "Flexible Kite" in 1956 and it was further developed and christened "sled" by Frank Scott. Ed Grauel has said, "Allison's place in the history of kiting is assured. He gave the world one of the simplest, yet one of the finest all-around kites that anyone has evolved in over 2,500 years of kiting."

Sleds are probably the most widely-used classroom kite design. There are many variations, plus a whole family of sleds with cells, Grauel's Bullet, Bushell's Flute and Greger's Hip Pocket Hybrid among them. The possibilities of this simple canopy with vertical longerons have not been exhausted. Some configurations need vents (holes) in the canopy for stability. The 36" sled is the standard. Smaller sleds fly well, and larger sleds can be temperamental.

Sled spars are on the front of the kite. The recommended bridle length is three or more times the width of the sled kite. Too short a bridle will prevent the kite from opening fully.

To wax line for sled kite bridles, check the notions counter at the fabric store for beeswax in a plastic dispenser. Kindergarten kids can use it by just running the line over the wax. It eliminates tangled bridles and resulting poor flight.

Kite Safety

1. Rain or storm comes up. Kites come down.
2. Kite pulls hard. Put on **gloves**.
3. A flying field is never over or on a public street or highway.
4. Power lines, antennas or airports too near. Find a new flying field. The sky is too crowded.
5. If you do lose your kite to a power line, call your utility company.
6. *Never* use metallic line and do not use metal in the construction of your kites.
7. Trees around? They eat kites.
8. Most of the time you will be looking up, not around. Know your flying field, wind direction and obstacles.
9. Spectators love to see your kites—small, large or controllable. Keep the kites and the people in a position to watch—not watch out!
10. Never discard tangled line on the field.

—*Ben-Franklin Kite Society*

Trashbag Sled Kite

1. To scale the modular measurements for plastic and fabric kites, multiply every figure in the pattern by the same number. For a 36" kite, multiply every number by 9. For a 16" kite, multiply by 4. Scale your sled kite by deciding on the elevation (the length of the spars). 16" or 24" kites make good use of both 48" dowels and standard trash bags. Divide the spar length by 4 (the module figure for the elevation) to get the multiplier for scaling.

2. With a draw-around pattern of half the kite, the canopies can be cut from unopened plastic or high-density polyethylene bags.

3. If the kite is over 16", use another strip of tape at the spar mid-point. The tape at the dowel tips should go up and over from the back of the kite to the front.

    Tie a dressmaker's knot (see Fabric Kites) in both ends of the bridle string so it will not slip out of the tape. Or tie loops and put tape through the loops (Stapled Sled.) The flying line ties through the loop in the center.

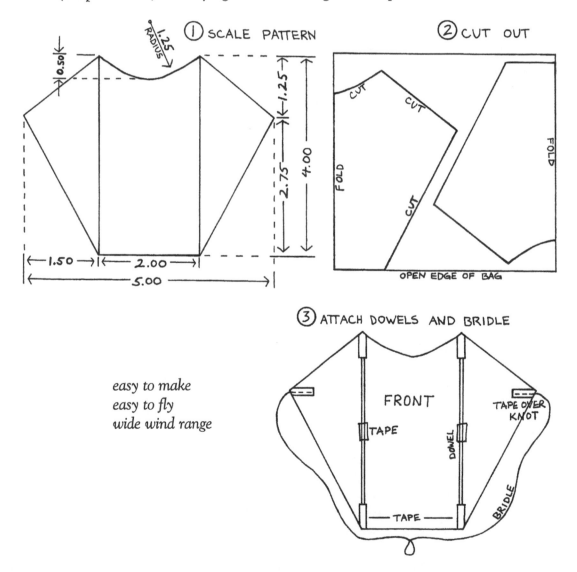

easy to make
easy to fly
wide wind range

Carol Master's Mini-Sled Kite

This little kite came to me from Carol Master, who developed it for her daughter's nursery school class. It is so easy and inexpensive that it makes group kitemaking and flying possible for everyone who can hold a string. I have used it in kindergarten and first-grade classes. Flown on thread, it can outfly heavier kites.

Carol used bread bags for her kites. The mini-sled also works well in high-density poly and in lightweight paper, gift wrap being a good choice. I use it as a greeting card in a legal-size envelope. A cardboard reel wound with thread will protect the straws from bending. GO FLY A KITE is an appropriate message.

Materials: lightweight plastic, about 8"x14"
two 7 3/4" plastic drinking straws
cellophane tape
45" crochet thread for bridle
scrap plastic for tail, 3/4"x5'

Tools: scissors or utility knife, punch or needle

Follow the diagrams to make the kite. The flying line ties through the loop in the center of the bridle. Add more tail for heavy winds. The pattern can be scaled for straws of other lengths.

easy to make
easy to fly
light/ medium wind

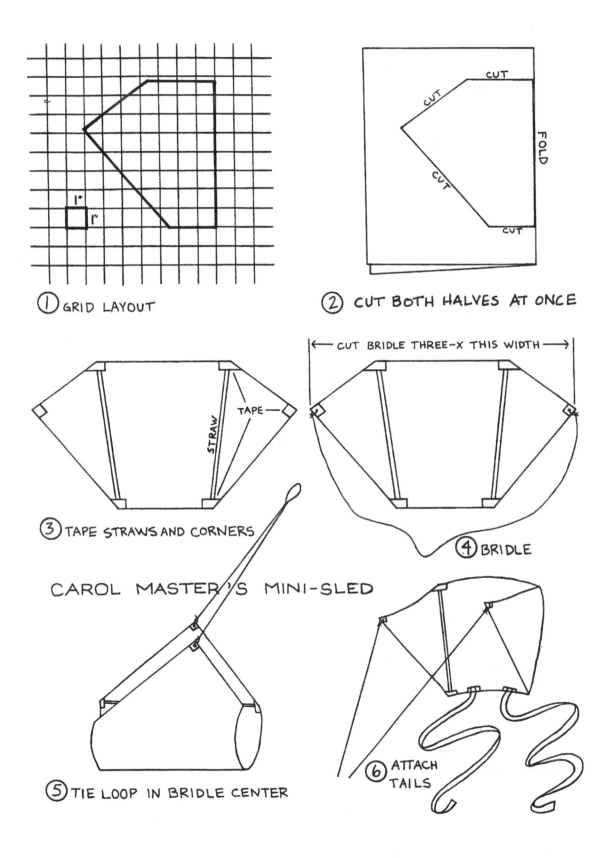

① GRID LAYOUT

② CUT BOTH HALVES AT ONCE

CUT
CUT
CUT
CUT
FOLD

③ TAPE STRAWS AND CORNERS

STRAW
TAPE

④ BRIDLE

← CUT BRIDLE THREE-X THIS WIDTH →

CAROL MASTER'S MINI-SLED

⑤ TIE LOOP IN BRIDLE CENTER

⑥ ATTACH TAILS

1"
1"

Stapled Sled Kite

The Stapled Sled is THE classroom kite. Teachers say, "We always have the material, anyone can make it, and it always flies!"

Sled kites, made with minimum materials and simple construction, are classroom favorites. With two patterns, butcher paper, string, tape and a stapler, the Stapled Sled is also the choice for ongoing, do-it-yourself, learning-center kitemaking.

The measurement of the vertical spar denotes the size of a sled kite. Stapled Sleds can be scaled down to 10" in lightweight paper, and up to 36", which may not be the upper limit, but is close to what stapled paper spars can sustain in a good wind. Sleds under 18" generally require tails for stabilization. Well-made larger Hornbeams fly well without tails. The Hornbeam is a sled variation by Guy Aydlett.

The diagrams are for a 24" Hornbeam, but any sled design can be easily tried in stapled paper. Cut the pattern and add an extension on the spar line–3" for a 24" kite, 4" for a 36". If you scale this kite, make the strip pattern one-half as wide as the spar area width.

Materials: tough, lightweight paper
strapping tape
bridle string, 3 times the finished width of the kite

 Tools: scissors, yardstick, pencil, stapler, marking pen

1.   Cut out and open up the kite. Lay the folding strip pattern on each wing in turn, matching A-A and B-B, and using the strip as a rule to draw the fold lines on the kite.

2.   Folding the wing towards the center of the kite, crease on the A-A line. Fold and crease again, bringing the first crease to meet the B-B line. Staple the folds at the ends and at 2" intervals.

3.   Tie a secure loop in each end of the bridle line and tape in place as shown. Find the center of the bridle and tie a loop. The flying line ties through this loop.

easy to make
easy to fly
wide wind range

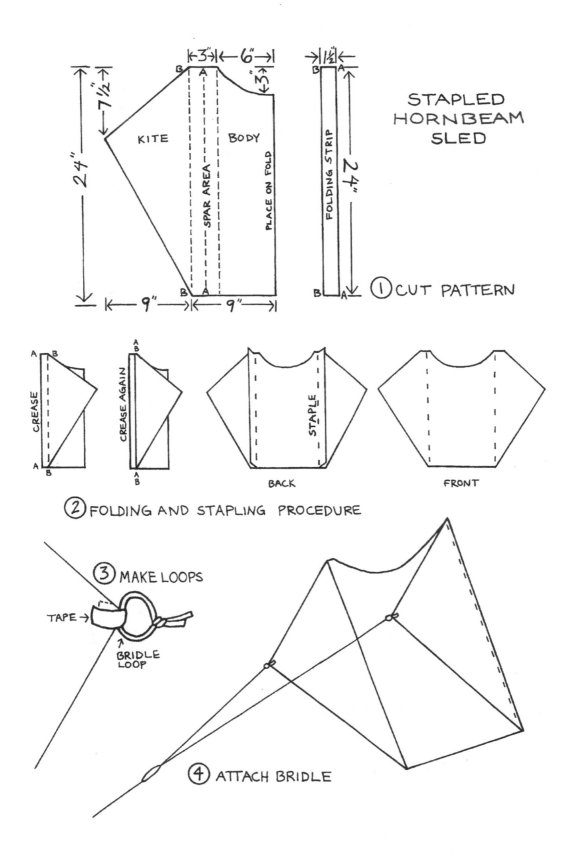

STAPLED
HORNBEAM
SLED

① CUT PATTERN

② FOLDING AND STAPLING PROCEDURE

③ MAKE LOOPS

④ ATTACH BRIDLE

Fabric Hornbeam Sled Kite

See the instructions for the Fabric Bullet for the general information on finishing the edges of fabric sleds. See Stapled Hornbeam Sled for dimensions.

Hemming or binding is done before sleeves are sewn. Though it goes against the grain for a dressmaker to put a seam on the front when it could be concealed, kitemakers generally recommend putting the spar sleeves on fabric sleds on the front rather than on the back. That is, bring wrong sides together when stitching the sleeve. Reinforce the tip ends of the sleeves with an extra layer of material before closing them. A 2" square of material will do.

Sleeve width: Multiply the diameter of the spar by four. Allow 1" for a 1/4" dowel. This forms a snug sleeve.

Reinforce the fin tips and insert eyelets or sew on loops for the bridle. Insert dowels, close sleeves and attach the bridle.

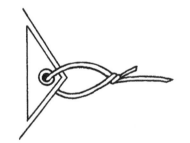

① EXTEND BASIC HORNBEAM FOR SLEEVES

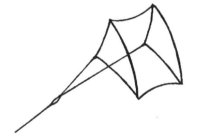

② BRING SLEEVE LINES TOGETHER AND STITCH

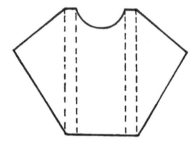

③ REINFORCE TIPS AND INSERT EYELETS

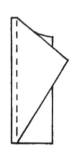

FABRIC HORNBEAM SLED

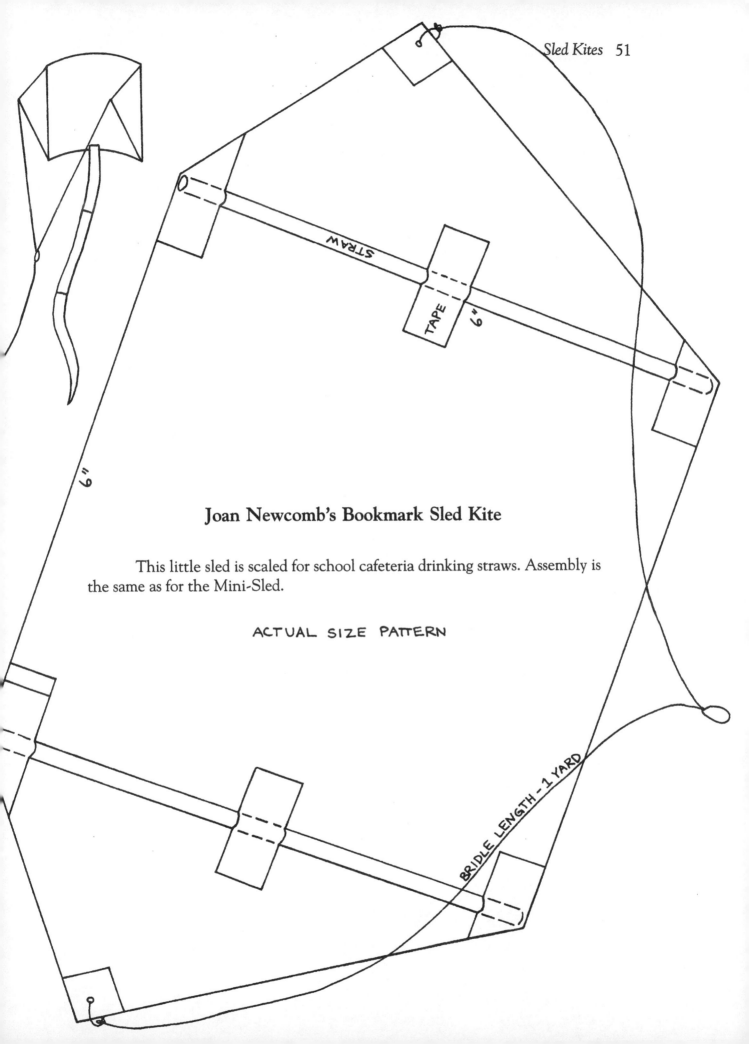

STRAW

TAPE

6"

6"

Joan Newcomb's Bookmark Sled Kite

This little sled is scaled for school cafeteria drinking straws. Assembly is the same as for the Mini-Sled.

ACTUAL SIZE PATTERN

BRIDLE LENGTH – 1 YARD

Bullet Kite

Ed Grauel developed and patented the Bullet in 1973. He was working to eliminate the wobble inherent in sled-type kites. The Bullet is a sled with cells on the back, a hybrid which combines a flat lifting surface with enclosed lifting surfaces.

The 26" Bullet (shown here in fabric) is what Ed calls "the most pleasing version." Scale larger or smaller Bullet kites from these dimensions. Use 50# test line for larger Bullets flying in heavy winds. The Bullet also flies well in light breezes. It is a sophisticated kite which is simple to make. "Patented" means don't make it to sell. Tails or a drogue are sometimes needed.

Mini-Bullet Kite

Made of tissue paper or a high-density poly bag, this Bullet is sparred by the tape which attaches the sleeves to the canopy. The sleeves have been widened by one-half inch per cell because they do not open as wide with the doublestick tape construction. Fly it on thread in light to medium winds.

Materials: tissue paper or high-density poly bag
1/2" wide doublestick tape
4' crochet thread for bridle
cellophane tape for bridle and tail attachment

Tools: scissors, marking pen, needle

Make a template from this full-size pattern. Trace around and cut out. Cut 1"x5' strip for tail.

For a 13" kite made in the same way, double all the measurements, with the two outer spars reinforced with matchstick bamboo laid on the doublestick between the sleeve and the kite face.

somewhat difficult to make
easy to fly
light winds

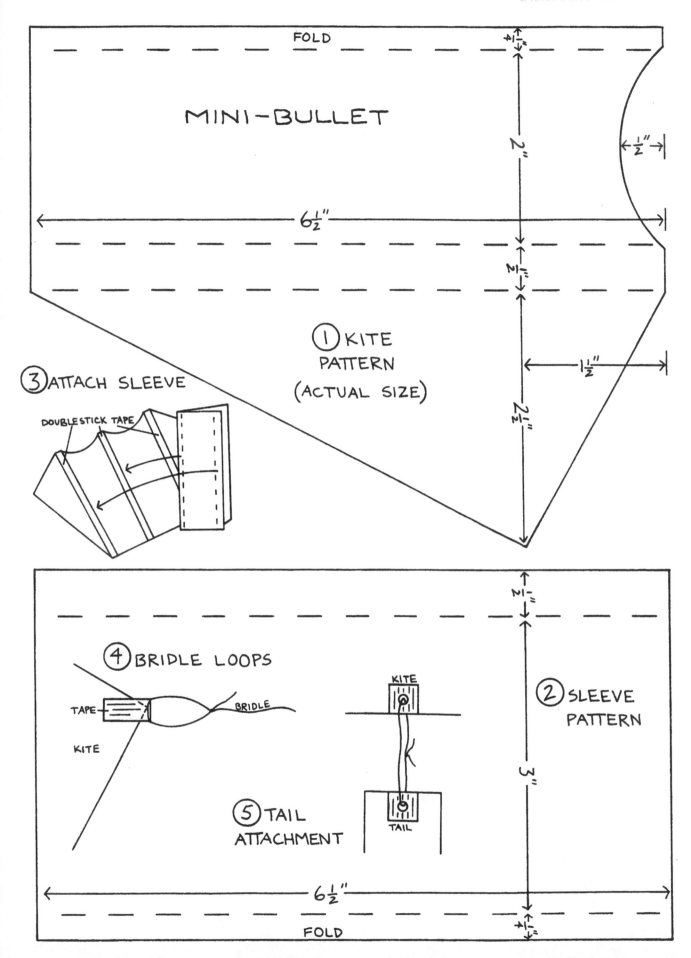

FOLD

MINI-BULLET

$\frac{1}{4}$"

2"

6$\frac{1}{2}$"

$\frac{1}{2}$"

$\frac{1}{2}$"

1$\frac{1}{2}$"

2$\frac{1}{2}$"

① KITE
PATTERN
(ACTUAL SIZE)

③ ATTACH SLEEVE

DOUBLESTICK TAPE

④ BRIDLE LOOPS

TAPE

BRIDLE

KITE

② SLEEVE
PATTERN

$\frac{1}{2}$"

3"

KITE

⑤ TAIL
ATTACHMENT

TAIL

6$\frac{1}{2}$"

$\frac{1}{4}$"

FOLD

Plastic Bullet Kite

The Plastic Bullet is a great classroom kite, new to your students and with the pull of a larger kite. This 24" classroom version of the Bullet is scaled to make efficient use of 4' dowels. Three dowels make two kites.

Materials: sheet plastic, 33 1/2"x24" and 19 1/2"x26"
three 3/16" dowels, 24" long
cellophane tape
doublestick tape
strapping tape
3 yards 30# test line

Tools: scissors, marking pen, punch

1-3.   Make the pattern, draw around it and cut out the kite and the cells.

4-5.   Tape the spars in place on the back of the kite. Lay doublestick tape on the center spar. Fold the cells on the center line, centering on the tape. Open the cells and press along the spar to seal. Join the outer edges of the cells to the kite with cello tape—one-half on the cell, one-half on the body of the kite.

Reinforce the spar tips and bridle as shown.

somewhat difficult to make
easy to fly
wide wind range

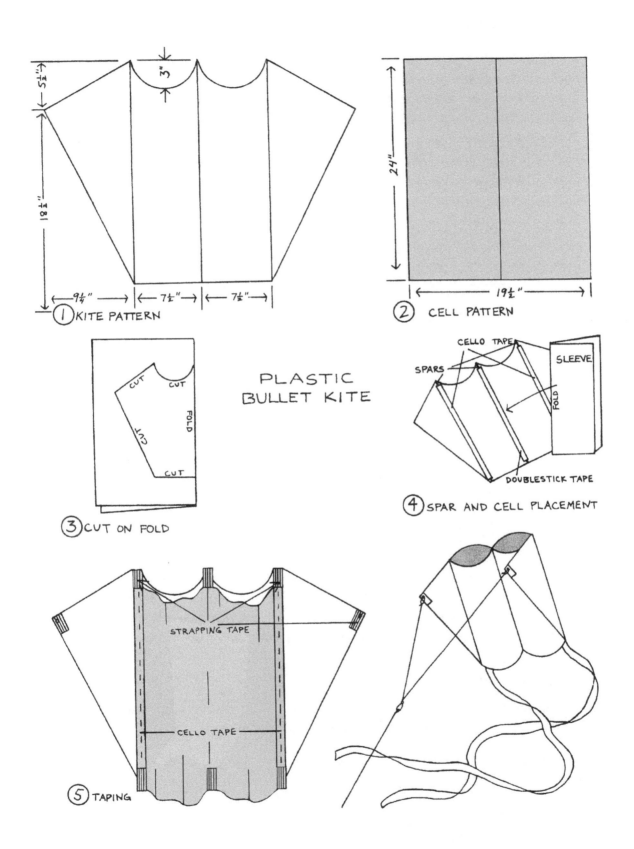

① KITE PATTERN

② CELL PATTERN

PLASTIC
BULLET KITE

③ CUT ON FOLD

④ SPAR AND CELL PLACEMENT

⑤ TAPING

Fabric Bullet Kite

There is much to be said for finishing sled edges simply by hot cutting. It's fast, it does not distort off-grain edges as stitching can do and it wears quite well. The edges may begin to fray with extended flight in strong winds, but for the time it takes, it is an easy, effective option. The edges may also be coated with Fray Check.

If I am making a kite for a show, I will hem or bind. Otherwise, my sleds (up to 36") and Bullets (up to 26") are finished with heat-sealed edges. For the smaller kites, the 13" fabric Bullet, and sleds under 24", heatsealing is the choice, because it does not add weight.

Use 1/2" or 5/8" polyester grosgrain ribbon or tape for binding. To bind, use your binding attachment or fold the ribbon in the middle the long way and press. Slip the edge of the kite into the fold and stitch. Reinforce the tip ends of the sleeves with an extra layer of material before closing them. A 2" square of material will do.

If you plan to hem the edges, add a 1/2" hem allowance when cutting. To minimize stretching, stitch on the fold line before folding the hem. Hemming is not practical on the curved edges at the top of the canopy. Bind or hot cut these. Hem or bind before assembling the kite.

Materials: sailcloth (measurements on diagram)
three 3/16" dowels, 26" long
1/2" or 5/8" poly ribbon for loops
3 yards 30# test line for bridle

1. Mark stitching lines on both canopy and cells for accuracy in joining the two pieces.

2-3. Turn under 1/4" on the outer edges of the cells. Match turned edges with the sleeve lines on the canopy and stitch. Stitching is across both ends and down both sides, breaking the stitching about 1" from the base on one side and leaving a 1" opening for spar insertion. This allows for easy replacement of a broken spar.

4-5. Sew on bridle and tail loops. Insert spars.

Cut all dimensions in half for a 13" fabric Bullet, which needs only the two outside spars. Stitch the cells to the canopy in the center.

somewhat difficult to make
easy to fly
wide wind range

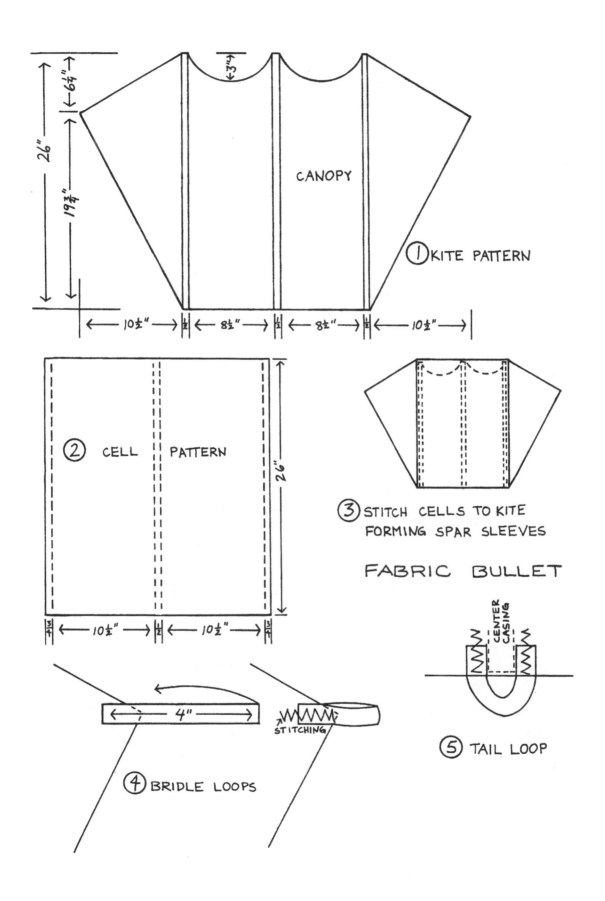

① KITE PATTERN

CANOPY

② CELL PATTERN

③ STITCH CELLS TO KITE FORMING SPAR SLEEVES

FABRIC BULLET

④ BRIDLE LOOPS

STITCHING

⑤ TAIL LOOP

CENTER CASING

Whole Bag Kite

High-density polyethylene shopping bags are crackly, lightweight, and may come in bright colors. They are ideal for this kite.

The idea for a classroom kite using the entire bag came from John Spendlove of England, who sent a sketch for the square kite. The design is scaled for kites 12" or under, small enough to be sparred with matchstick bamboo reed. Bigger bags and bags with gussets can be used by cutting away the sealed bottom edge and trimming the bag to the desired width. Ideally, the bag material should be two to three times as long as it is wide, providing for a generous fringe.

The width of the bag can be the unit, or module, with the other measurements derived from it. Six-inch square kites are successful fliers. For classrooms, I go to 12" square, still a little kite, to be flown on thread.

Three-Legged Bridle

A bridle attached to the kite at two points, as on the Eddy Kite, is a two-point bridle. Square kites fly better with three-point bridles, which balance the kite and distribute the force of the wind throughout the frame. Balancing and adjusting a three-point bridle can be difficult. John Spendlove introduced me to this double-loop version.

Some guidelines on bridle length: On small kites, it is best to make the lines relatively long, starting with two times the length of the diagonal, since knots take up as much line in the bridle for a small kite as they do in a larger one. The finished bridle on squares 12" and under should stand away from the kite face by a measurement equivalent to one-half the length of the diagonal. Any extra bridle length may be taken up in the loop.

I bridle small squares with needle and thread. From the face side of the kite, pull the thread down and up over one spar and down and up over the spar intersection, leaving a loop of thread between. Tie off both ends and repeat the process for the other side. (Since the lines meet at the intersection, you can do this with a single length of thread, knotted after the formation of the first loop, then proceeding to the second.)

You now have two bridle loops of equal length (4). Tie these together in a single loop, which forms the towing point. The angle shown in (5), in which the plane formed by the top legs of the bridle is perpendicular to the face of the kite, will be right for most squares.

Whole Bag Kite

Materials: high-density polyethylene bag
matchstick bamboo reed
cellophane tape
thread

Tools: scissors, needle, ruler

1.   Split the bag up the sides. If there is a seam flap at the base of the bag, it will become part of the fringe. Fold and tape a 3/4" hem at one end (top of the kite.)

2.   Square the kite face by folding as shown.

3.   Measure the diagonal and mark the bridle points. Reinforce with tape. Tape the spars in place with tape running front to back over the spar tips.

4.   Cut the fringe.

5.   Turn the kite over. Bridle. See three-legged bridle discussion for length.

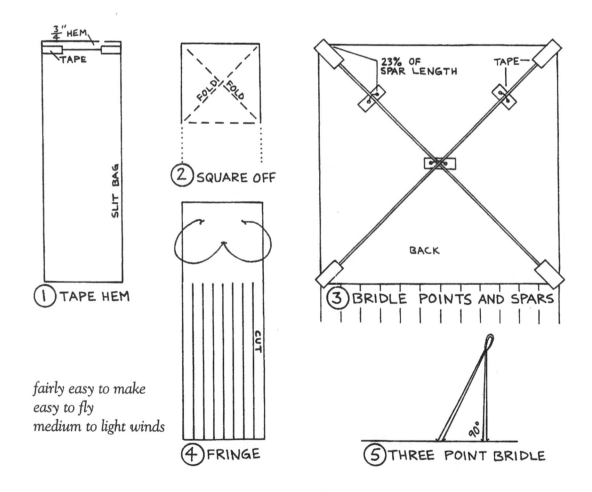

fairly easy to make
easy to fly
medium to light winds

Plastic Fantasmo Kite

This 17"-square plastic kite with a 24" diagonal can be framed with one 4' dowel and a high or low-density plastic bag.

Flat kites generally require tails for stable flight. Part of the Fantasmo's charm is the long, undulating tail, which may be left in a pennon-like strip or sliced to ribbons. The ribbon slices seem to work better for fabric kites.

Each finished square kite may differ slightly in the precise length of the diagonal. Adjust the length of the spar accordingly.

If you are using the Fantasmo as a classroom kite, there are advantages to making a pattern and working over it to make the kite, since this method makes possible the easy, accurate transfer of measurements. (See the Joseph Lee Delta Kite.) For a single kite, make the measurements directly on the plastic.

Materials: plastic, about 1 mil thick, slightly larger than 17"x20"
3/16" dowel, 4' long, cut in half
cellophane tape, strapping tape
string for bridle
20' of 6" wide plastic for tail

Tools: scissors, punch, ruler, needle, marking pen

1. Tape the pattern to the working surface. Tape the plastic over the pattern. Mark the fold lines and the bridle points.

2. Run tape along the long (top and bottom) edges of the kite. Reinforce the bridle points with tape. Cut out the kite.

3. Fold the sides over as shown. Close the ends with strapping tape to form the spar sleeves. Insert the spars. Poke holes for the bridle.

4-5. **TURN KITE OVER.** Cut three 24" lengths of string, two for the bridle and one for a tail halter. Bridle the kite and attach the tail as shown. Stiffen the top edge of the tail with a scrap of dowel.

fairly difficult to make
easy to fly
medium winds

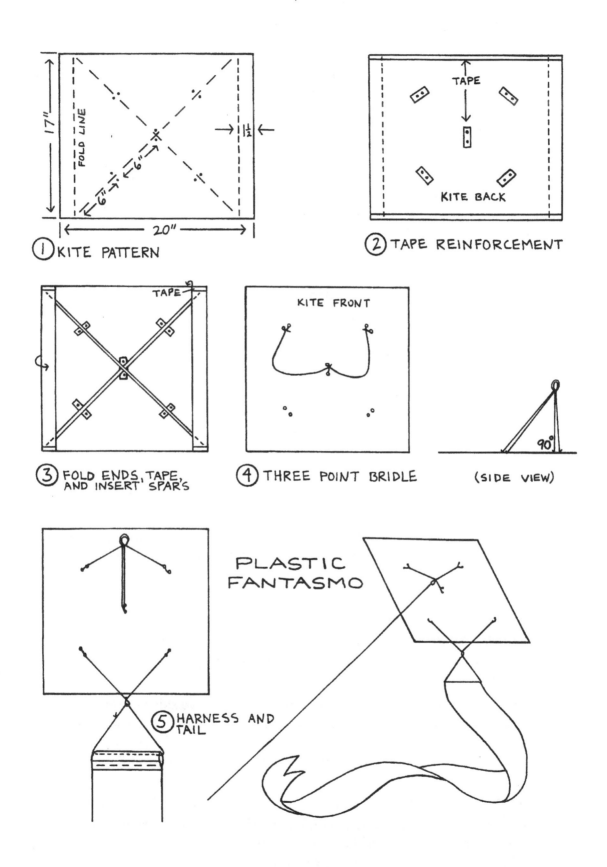

① KITE PATTERN

② TAPE REINFORCEMENT

③ FOLD ENDS, TAPE, AND INSERT SPARS

④ THREE POINT BRIDLE

(SIDE VIEW)

⑤ HARNESS AND TAIL

PLASTIC FANTASMO

Fabric Square Kite and Square Diamond Kite

A hemmed fabric square with x-frame spars can be flown square with the world like the Fantasmo. It will need about 60 feet of tail streamers. The Square Diamond is framed with a vertical spine and a curved spar arching across the horizontal. It flies on point, like a dancer. The squares can be multi-colored quilt blocks, stabilized by stitching the patches to a crisp interfacing backing, and designed to decorate the wall or the sky.

The fiberglass spar of the Diamond can be removed and the kite rolled to bag. Flat envelope bags protect squares and make them easier to store and to transport. Gather tail streamers in pleats and secure with rubber bands for storage. Don't cut the spars until you have hemmed the the fabric square because lengths can vary from one kite to another.

Square Diamond Kite Instructions

Materials: 28" fabric square
reinforcements, may be self-adhesive fabric
1/4" dia. dowel, about 37" long
3/16" dia. fiberglass rod, about 44 1/2" long, with end caps for the tips
1 1/2 yards 5/8" poly grosgrain ribbon
l yard 30# braided line for bridle
small split ring

1.   Stitch one-half inch from all edges. Turn and press on the stitching line. Turn the free edge under and stich the hem.

2.   Cut two 5" lengths of ribbon. Seal the ends by hot cutting or by passing them through a candle flame. Fold and stitch in place as shown, forming a pocket. The spar slips between the two layers of ribbon. Use 16" lengths of ribbon for the side pockets. Stitch pockets to kite.

3-4.   Tails may be attached with eyelets or narrow ribbon loops at the outer corners and at the base. Reinforce before inserting eyelets. Stitch loops in place. Measure and cut dowel for the spine. It should be snug without stretching. Sand the tips.

Hold one end of the fiberglass rod at the lower end of a side pocket. Curve it to the opposite corner, intersecting the center spar about 7 1/2" from the tip. Cut the rod to size, cap the tips, slip it behind the spine and insert the tips in the pockets. Reinforce the bridle points at the intersection and 8" up from the base.

5.   **TURN KITE OVER.** Bridle from the front. Thread a needle and go down and up, tying one end of the line around the spar intersection and the other over the spine. Set the bridle as shown. A split ring fastened to the bridle with a larkshead knot makes it readily adjustable.

6-7. Tails—one of many possibilities and a good way to use up scraps. I cut, stitch together, and hem about 60 feet of 3"-wide material in random colors if my kite is multi-colored. This is cut into shorter streamers, allowing about 15' to each side and 30' to the base. I make them in bundles of two or three streamers, finishing the ends as shown and attaching them to the kite by means of swivels and eyelets.

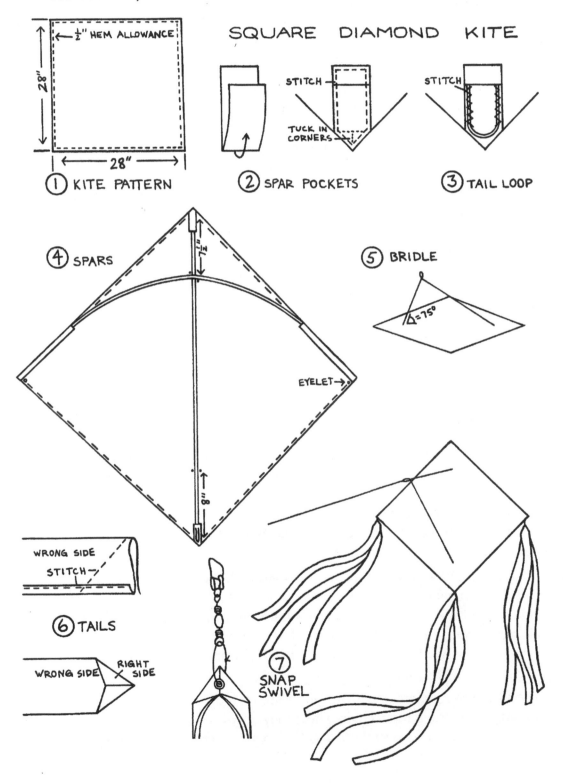

SQUARE DIAMOND KITE

① KITE PATTERN

② SPAR POCKETS

③ TAIL LOOP

④ SPARS

⑤ BRIDLE

⑥ TAILS

⑦ SNAP SWIVEL

Eddy Kites

The Eddy Kite is a classic, patented in 1900 by William Eddy, who reinvented the bowed, tailless kite of Malaya. It was used to lift instruments by the U. S. Weather Service, and a train of ten Eddy kites reached a height of 23,385 feet in 1910 at Mount Weather, Virginia, a high-flying record which stood for many years. In the Eddy formula the crosspiece is the same length as the vertical spar, and they are joined at a point one-fifth of the way down the vertical. Properly balanced, bridled and bowed, it flies without a tail.

Precision is important when building a traditional Eddy Kite and I do not recommend it as a First Kite for beginners, since I believe the conviction many people have that kites are difficult to make and hard to fly stems from negative experience with two-stick kites. Students can proceed with confidence to the Eddy when they have had success with more tolerant kites.

Construction is not difficult but it cannot be haphazard, and field adjustments are almost always needed. A little experimenting will put every kite into the air. The Eddy Kite can be scaled up to very large sizes. 24" and 36" kites are practical, easy to transport and to work with in the classroom.

Old-time kites were made with sticks and, if I am teaching the Eddy as an historical kite, I will try to arrange with a school shop instructor for kite sticks, which should be notched at both ends. 3/16" dowels can be substituted for 24" to 30" kites. Lightweight kraft paper is a good choice for the cover. Gift wrap is good, butcher paper too heavy and tissue paper may be used for smaller kites in light winds.

Conover Eddy Kite

A glance at the table of contents of this book gives the reader a look at the variety possible in a single kite design. One of the pleasures of kitemaking is meeting an old friend–in the case of the Eddy, an old standby–in new dress. When that new edition is the kite reduced to its essence, as is the case with the Conover Eddy, making it an ideal classroom kite, it is welcomed, not just with open arms, but with eager hands.

Leonard Conover of the Greater Delaware Valley Kite Society says he developed this kite when he grew tired of making deltas out of bedsheets. His efforts, beginning with bedsheets, ended with plastic bags and a recipe which calls for one bag, one dowel and four pieces of tape. The genius touches are the pre-formed cross spar and the single bridle point, which insure that every kite will fly.

Conover bows his dowels by bundling a dozen with tape or rubber bands on the ends, holding them under the faucet for a minute, and slipping them between the rungs of a dining room chair, where they dry overnight. They emerge with a 5" bow, which soon relaxes to about 2 1/2". When I teach kites at summer camp, I put the center of the bundle behind a rafter with wooden blocks under each end and dampen them with a spray bottle. Some people arrange them around the pegs in the dishwasher. It is not necessary to soak the dowels, moistening them is sufficient.

Here is a simple dowel-bending jig:

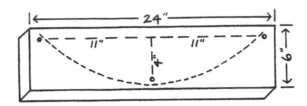

Kite Trains

Because it is small and easy to make and to handle, the Conover Eddy is probably the most popular kite in the country for assembling into a kite train. Great strings of Conovers, each numbering in the hundreds of kites, fly at the Long Beach, Washington, Festival every year. They are a grand sight, stairsteps to heaven. On an overcast day, the trains can look like sutures, stitches holding the sky together.

Trains, however, are not child's play and children should not be encouraged to build them. This small kite, one of which can be flown on crochet thread, needs heavy line for security as the number of kites builds. 150#-200# test line is recommended. The kites are spaced at approximately 5' intervals, measured by extending the arms fully. It could be somewhat less, but each kite needs its own air space, called "clean air."

Because kite tails can foul the flying line, keep them short. Two 4' streamers are better than one 8'.

How are long trains of kites stored, fed into the wind and retrieved? Find a cardboard box, big enough to hold the flat kites and layer them in carefully, to be fed out one by one. Some fliers of trains have put wheels or rollers on the boxes.

Always wear gloves when flying kite trains and other strong-pulling kites. It is a good idea to have a strong anchor line attached to the kite line about 10' from the bottom (closest to the flier) kite. Fasten the line to the anchor before you start letting out kites.

Conover Eddy Kite

Materials: trash bag (two diamonds or one fringed Conover can be cut
from a tall kitchen bag, 22"x24")
two 1/8" dowels, 24" long
cellophane tape or self-sticking labels
small rubber band

Alternate materials: A high-density polyethylene bag may be used.
Self-sticking labels make spar attachment easy.

Tools: scissors, marking pen

1.   Preform the cross spar. Make the pattern and place it on the folded edge of the
unopened bag. Trace around it and cut out.

Fringed Conover: Lay the diamond pattern on the plastic after tracing around
the fringed pattern. Draw the bottom (trailing edge) line of the diamond,
establishing the limit of the fringe. Slice through both layers to cut out the
kite and the fringe.

2.   Join the spars with a small rubber band as shown. Open the kite and tape the
cross spar in place, then the spine.

3-4.   The flying line ties directly to the spar intersection. Add tails to the diamond.

easy to make
easy to fly
light/medium winds

To cut plastic, barely open the scissors. Begin cutting while pushing
lightly against the plastic, which is held taut by tape or by hand. The blades
should slice through the plastic. Practice on scraps.

To cut a dowel, roll the stick under a knife blade, scoring all around.
It will snap on the scored line.

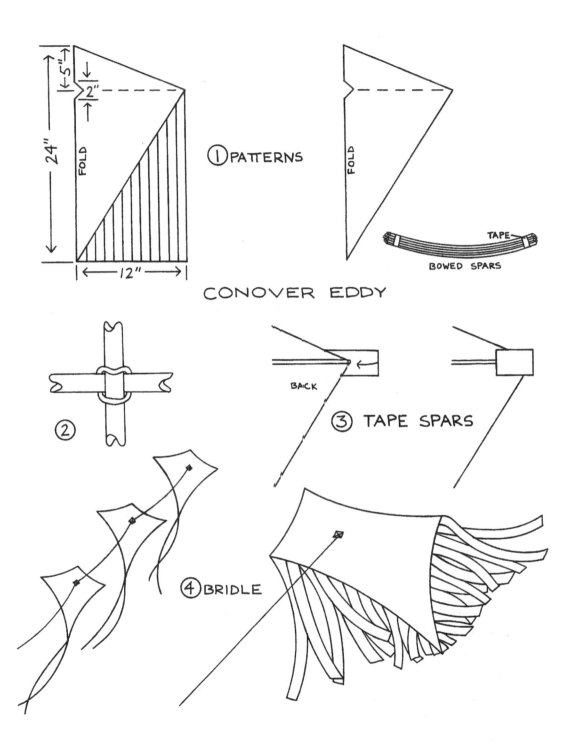

① PATTERNS

FOLD

24"

5"

2"

12"

TAPE

BOWED SPARS

CONOVER EDDY

②

③ TAPE SPARS

BACK

④ BRIDLE

Traditional Eddy Kite

Once upon a time, the standard ingredients in a kite recipe were paper, framing string, wooden sticks, and mucilage or flour-and-water paste. The methods of construction shown here—lashing the spars together, reinforcing and defining the outline of the kite with framing string, then holding the whole together with paste—were standard for box, flat and bowed kites in kitemaking instructions published before 1960. Such kites as the Winged Box and the French Military can also be made in this way, and quite simply, too, if modern gluestick is used and tape is added to the list of ingredients. I include these instructions to introduce modern kitemakers to traditional techniques and materials.

Eddy Kite Instructions

Materials: tough lightweight paper to cover
2 kite sticks, 3/16"x1/4"x36", notched at both ends
   or use 3/16" dowels
30# test line for framing, bridle, bowstring
tape for reinforcing bridle holes
gluestick

Tools: yardstick, ruler, pencil, scissors

1.   Make the frame by marking the midpoint of the cross spar and a point 7" down from the top of the longeron. Join the sticks at right angles. Glue and lash the spars together (1a).

   Tie a loop at one end of the framing string, and slip it through the notch at the top. With the cross spar underneath, weave the string in each notch in turn, coming up from the bottom, wrapping around twice, and going down from the top, keeping the framing string on the underside of the frame all the way around (1b). A paper square will help maintain right angles. Tie a knot at each corner to hold the shape.

   Cross spar underneath, lay the frame on the paper. Using a straight edge, draw the outline of the kite around the framing string. Trim, leaving a 3/4" flap. Crease the flaps over the string and trim the excess at the corners. Glue the flaps down.

2.   The bridle should be one and one-half times the vertical length of the kite. Bridle from the front, down and up over the crossed sticks. The lower end of the bridle ties through the notch at the base.

3.   Cut the bowstring six inches longer than the cross spar. Tie a loop in one end of the bowstring. Have one person bend the cross spar while another slips the loop over the notch at one end and ties the other end through the opposite notch. The bow should be 3"-5" deep and can be adjusted for light or heavy winds. Also see Button Tensioner for adjusting the bow (3a). This requires a longer string.

Slip the bowstring loop out of the notch and store the kite flat. The bridle angle for the Eddy Kite must fit the wind of the day. Hold the bridle by one finger and see what the wind wants. Use a split ring or string loop for easy adjustment. Fly on 30#-50# test line. Well-made Eddy kites fly without a tail, but if adjustments in bow and bridle are not sufficient, a tail will give needed stability.

somewhat difficult to make
may need tuning to fly
wide wind range

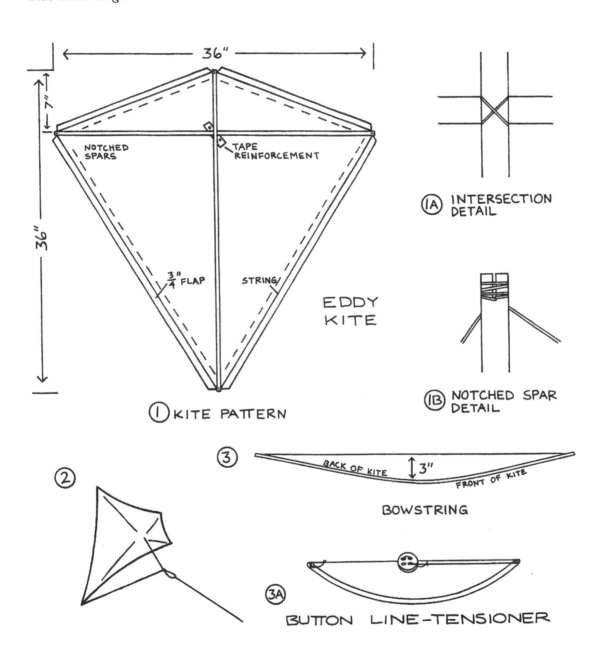

EDDY KITE

① KITE PATTERN

NOTCHED SPARS

TAPE REINFORCEMENT

¾" FLAP

STRING

ⒶA INTERSECTION DETAIL

ⒷB NOTCHED SPAR DETAIL

②

③ BACK OF KITE   3"   FRONT OF KITE

BOWSTRING

③A BUTTON LINE-TENSIONER

Eddy Bird Kite

Make Lee Toy's Eddy Bird Kite, also a favorite for kite trains, following the instructions for the plastic Conover Eddy Kite.

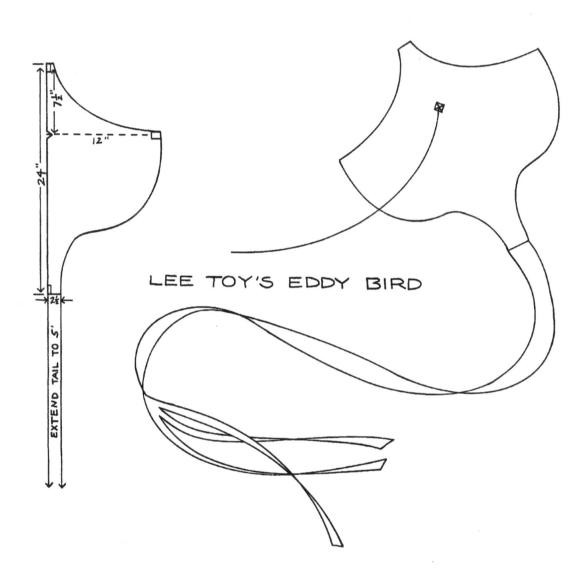

LEE TOY'S EDDY BIRD

Delta Kite

Every kiteflier needs a delta for the days when the wind is barely breathing. Because of the floating spar construction, with none of the spars attached to each other, the wing is shaped by the wind–shaped from moment to moment, in fact, as the wind varies. A delta can be sustained in the air by walking with it and, if light-weight materials are used, a three mile-per-hour wind will lift it into the sky. Though deltas will fly in higher winds, their basic element is the mere breeze.

The delta patterns scale directly and very large delta kites have been made and flown. Because it is a soaring kite, moving on instead of against the wind as do box and flat kites, the pull is relatively light. However, a big delta in a strong wind should be flown on a heavy line and handled with gloves.

The delta is everyone's choice for light-to-no-wind days and, when deltas are made for this purpose, they can be sparred with dowels a shade lighter than would be regarded as normal for a particular size, 3/16" dowels for a kite with a 60" base, for example. Replace them if they become warped after some hours of flying. A 75"-base kite is the largest which can be sparred with 4' long dowels. Fiberglass and graphite rods may be used in larger deltas. They are heavier than wood.

The 60" delta may also be made in plastic, following the instructions for the Little Delta or the Zephyr and using tape generously.

Tails, fringe, drogues or spinners may be added for decoration. They are usually not required for stability.

Spreader Bar Options

Decide early in the construction of the delta what method you will use to attach the spreader bar. Tape- and-ring attachment is done before the side sleeves are closed. So are the other tabs. A loop of string or tape which goes around the center spar and which the spreader bar slips through will restrain the spreader and maintain the delta shape in heavier winds. The loop should be 2"-4" deep.

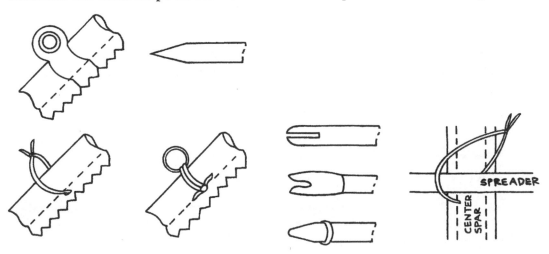

Little Delta Kite

I live in delta country, in an area with little or no wind much of the time, making this half-size, open-keel delta a frequent choice for classroom use. The design has been refined with suggestions from many young kitemakers, and the fringed apron and open keel insure that every kite will fly. The Little Delta weighs less than an ounce. Tail streamers can be added to increase its flying range or to correct the rare unstable kite.

Working over a pattern taped to the table makes framing small delta kites easy. I carry a bundle of patterns, one for each kitemaker, to the classroom. Each kite requires about three yards of cellophane tape, 2' of doublesided tape, and 1" of strapping tape. Three 4'-long dowels make two kites.

When I prepare for a class, I bundle a dozen dowels together and cut the two 14" and one 17" lengths on the band saw. Spreader bars are measured and cut to fit.

This pattern can be scaled to double the size by doubling all dimensions for a 60" base, a great flier. Use 3/16" dowels, with a 1/4" dowel for the spreader bar.

Little Delta Kite Instructions

Materials: tall kitchen trash bag
2 dowels, 1/8"x4'
cellophane tape
doublesided tape
strapping tape or mailing labels
plastic drinking straw

Tools: scissors, utility knife, punch

1.   Tape the pattern to the working surface. Lay the plastic over the pattern and tape in place, allowing for fringe at the base.

2-3. Cut one 17" and two 14" dowels. Tape the 17" dowel in the center and the 14" dowels on the leading edges, running the tape all the way to the tip.

Fold the flap at the base of the kite in half and cut the fringe as shown. Cut out the kite and the keel, running the scissors along the edge of the tape which covers the dowels.

Cut two 1 1/2" lengths of plastic drinking straw. Form a sleeve by folding one end over and sealing with tape. The end of the straw must be closed or the spreader bar will poke through in flight. Tape the sleeves FIRMLY in place.

TURN KITE OVER and realign over pattern lines.

4.   Lay doublesided tape on the keel placement lines. Lay the long outside edges of the keel on the tape and press firmly to adhere. Reinforce with cellophane tape over the outside edges.

5. Fold strapping tape over the nose of the keel. Punch the hole for the flying line through the tape. **TURN KITE OVER.**

6. Measure and cut the spreader bar to size from the remaining dowel. The kite should be rigid but not taut, the spreader running from the back of one sleeve to the back of the other. Insert the spreader in the sleeves.

fairly easy to make
easy to fly
light to medium winds

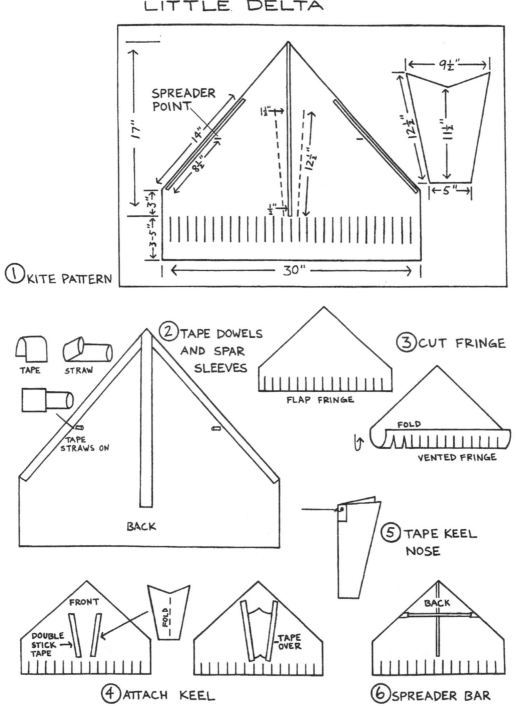

LITTLE DELTA

① KITE PATTERN
② TAPE DOWELS AND SPAR SLEEVES
③ CUT FRINGE
④ ATTACH KEEL
⑤ TAPE KEEL NOSE
⑥ SPREADER BAR

One-Piece Delta Kite

The One-Piece is my all time favorite classroom delta, easy to make and fly. For that reason, I am including it here even though it is also in *More Kites for Everyone*.

Materials: tall kitchen trash bag, 24"x30"
two 1/8"x4' dowels, cut thus: spine, 24"; two side spars, 19";
   one spreader, 18"
cellophane tape and strapping tape, both 3/4" wide
1" of plastic tubing, 1/8" inner diameter, cut into fourths
toothpick

Tools: yardstick, scissors, utility knife, 1/8" diameter punch, marking pen

1.   Draft pattern. Slit open the bottom of the bag. Lay the pattern on the fold (closed sides of the bag). One bag makes two kites. Cut out. With kite still folded, mark the center line on one side and the spreader spot on both sides.

2.   Fold the keel on the center line, crease. Carefully open one wing to the fold line and tape wings together as shown (keel is double.) You are working on the back of the kite with the keel on the front.

3.   Attach the spine and side spars by covering with tape.

4.   Cut three 2 1/2" lengths of strapping tape for the keel tip and the spreader attachments. Reinforce with a short piece of toothpick laid in the fold before the tape is doubled over. Punch holes as shown. Plastic washers on the ends of the spreader maintain the wingspread while allowing adjustment.

easy to make
easy to fly
light winds

To remove a plastic washer from a dowel, push it off instead of trying to pull it. Pulling only tightens the hold of the plastic on the wood. A clip clothespin makes a good pusher.

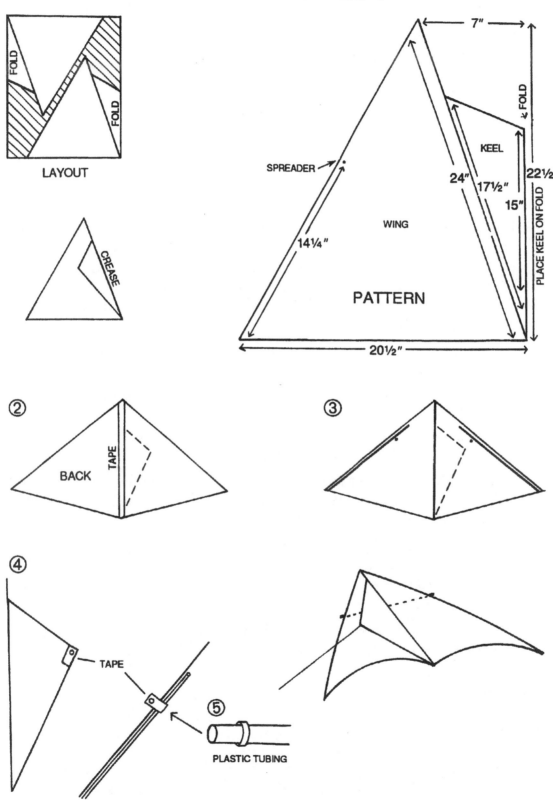

ONE-PIECE DELTA

LAYOUT

CREASE

7"

FOLD

KEEL

SPREADER

24" 17½"

15"

22½"

PLACE KEEL ON FOLD

14¼"

WING

PATTERN

20½"

② BACK TAPE

③

④ TAPE

⑤ PLASTIC TUBING

Tony Cyphert's Delta Kite

Tony Cyphert's deltas are scaled by the formula given in diagram (1).

Materials: Plastic or high density poly bag
dowels of appropriate size, 1/8" or 3/16"dia.
3/4" wide cellophane tape
3/4" wide strapping tape
3 1/2" plastic tubing for connectors
toothpick

Tools: Scissors, yardstick, marking pen, protractor, punch

When using Tony's formula to scale a delta for a particular-size bag remove the bottom seam. If the bag has a gusset, pull it out and flatten the bag. Measure the width. This is the basic measurement, determining the height of the kite, the 100% figure of the formula. Because the bag is folded, the base of the opened-out kite will be 200%. The drawing shows a kite made from a tall kitchen trash bag, 24" wide. Measurements are scaled and rounded off and 6" is allowed for a fringe. A 24" kite can be framed with 1/8" dowels.

Keel: Draw the long (79%) edge first. Mark the 60° angle at the tip and draw the 33% edge. Connect the lines to close the triangle.

1.   Cut out the kite, fringe, and mark the spreader points on both sides. Leave the kite folded. The keel is a single layer. Run tape inside all edges of the keel. Cut it out, slicing along the taped edges. Reinforce the tip with strapping tape or a label, placing a short length of toothpick in the fold.

2.   Line up the kite and the keel as shown. Join with tape at the top, bottom and about every 2" along the length. Flip the assembly and match the tape on the other side. This is the front of the kite.

3.   Open the wings and flatten the kite so you are working on the back. Tape the connectors in place on the side spars as shown. Tape the spine and side spars in place. Tacking the dowels in place with short lengths of tape before covering makes it easier.

Cut the spreader about 1" shorter than the distance across the kite at the spreader points.

easy to make
easy to fly
light to medium winds

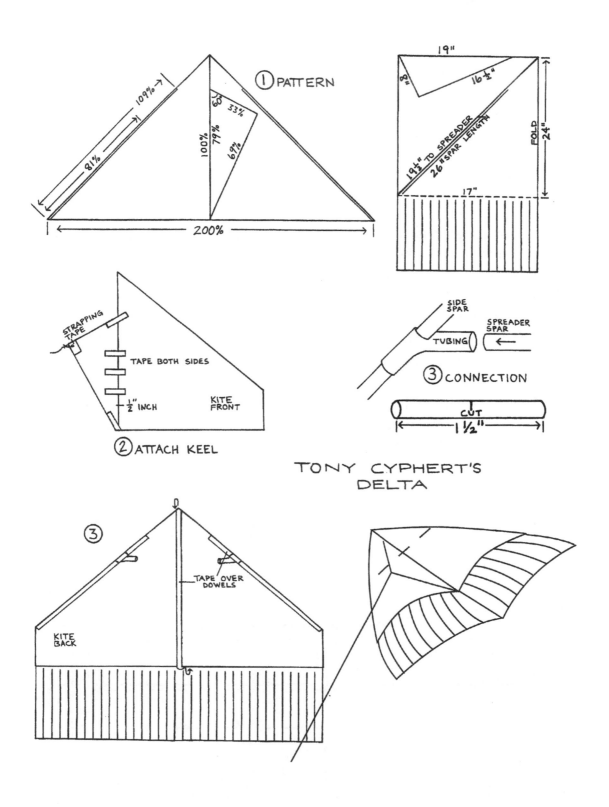

① PATTERN

109% → 100% 79% 33% 69% 60° 81% 200%

19" 8" 16½" FOLD 24" 19½" TO SPREADER 26" SPAR LENGTH 17"

② ATTACH KEEL

STRAPPING TAPE TAPE BOTH SIDES ½" INCH KITE FRONT

③ CONNECTION

SIDE SPAR SPREADER SPAR TUBING CUT 1½"

TONY CYPHERT'S DELTA

③

TAPE OVER DOWELS

KITE BACK

Joseph Lee's Delta Bird Kite

Joseph C. W. Lee is a Korean-American and a Methodist minister. I met him and the Delta Bird when he gave a workshop in a local church in the late seventies. It is an exceptionally fine kite, floating at a high angle on the lightest breeze, and in winds up to 12 mph. It is one of my all-time favorite kites.

The Delta Bird is relatively difficult to make, best suited to adults and older kids and fitting well into arts and crafts classes. Proceed carefully so your Bird is symmetrical and balanced. It introduces another method of making a kite, that is, by working over a pattern taped to the table. I carry a bundle of patterns, one for each kitemaker, to the classroom. I lay out the master pattern from the dimensions on the grid. Outline with marking pen, and trace copies by placing butcher paper on top and using a yardstick to keep the lines true. Non-woven interfacing from the fabric store is another durable pattern material.

Drawing the grid: A standard 8 1/2"x11" sheet of paper is a good substitute for a framing square. Draw the spine first. To achieve right angles, lay the paper at the measured points and line your yardstick up with it for the horizontals.

Plastic tubing for connectors is sold by the foot in hardware stores. Take a scrap of dowel along to check for a snug fit. The freezer bag is specified for the keel because it is stiffer than the trash bag.

When you cut out the kite with the scissors running along the taped edges, be careful not to cut the pattern as well. A snap clothespin makes a good pusher to remove dowels from tubing.

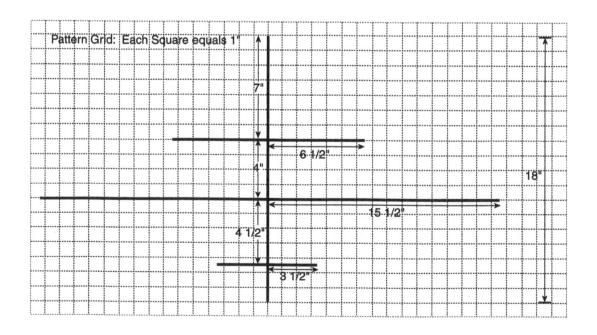

Pattern for Delta Bird Kite

Materials: tall kitchen trash bag
gallon size plastic freezer bag (Ziploc®) for keel
three 1/8" dia. dowels, 4' long: Cut one 27" spine, four 23 1/4"
    wing spars, one 18" spreader (spreader length is approximate, cut
    after kite is finished)
6" plastic tubing, 1/8" inner diameter, cut in four 1 1/2" segments
1/2" wide cellophane tape
about 1" of 3/4" wide strapping tape for reinforcing tie-on

Tools: pattern paper, yardstick, framing square, craft knife, scissors, punch,
pencil, black marking pen, needle and thread, clothespin

Preparations: Tape the pattern to the table. Slit the tall kitchen bag down one
side and across the end, the freezer bag on two sides. Open the
bags flat, and tape the single layers of plastic over the outline.
Do not cut the kite out yet.

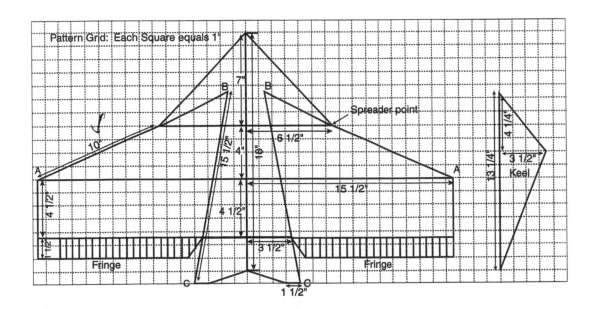

Delta Bird Kite Instructions

1.   **Wing spars:** Cut a notch in the center of two pieces of the tubing. Lay two of the 23 1/4" sticks on the outer edges and mark the spreader points. Insert the sticks in the tubing as shown. Join the outer wing spars and the inner wing spars with the unnotched tubing. Leave a little space between the sticks so the inverted "V" which they form bends easily.

2.   Place the spine on the center line. Secure it with small pieces of tape before covering the whole length. Smooth the tape down over the dowel. Beginning with the outer (leading) edges, tape the wing spars in place. Pull the inner wing spars to the lines and tape. Do not tape over the tubing. Run tape inside the line along the top edges of the kite and the upper edge of the fringe.

     The tape which covers the dowels will lap over the outline on the leading edges. Cut out the bottom and side edges of the kite. Cut the fringe in 1" wide segments. This is easier to do before the kite is completely cut out. Now cut along the tape to free the kite.

3.   Outline the short edges of the keel with tape inside the lines. Cut out. Reinforce the tip with strapping tape as shown. Punch a hole for the tie-on. **TURN KITE OVER.** Fold the wings back and crease to make an edge along the spine. Line the keel up with the spine and tape as shown. Turn the assembly over and tape along the other side. Trim the tape at top and bottom as needed.

4.   Insert the spreader ends in the tubing, and mark where the spine crosses the spreader. For a good dihedral, cut the spreader about 1" shorter than the length which would hold the kite flat. Starting from the back, insert the needle and thread next to the spine, through the keel, and back through the kite on the other side of the spine. Tie the ends of the string together to form a loop about 1 1/2" deep. The spreader slips through the loop. The Delta Bird is ready to fly.

     Surveyor's tape or plastic streamers cut from scraps make good tails, if desired. If the spine and wing spars and the top edges are outlined with black electrician's tape on the front of the kite (not the spar side) the resemblance to a bird is emphasized.

somewhat difficult to make
easy to fly
light to medium winds

DELTA BIRD

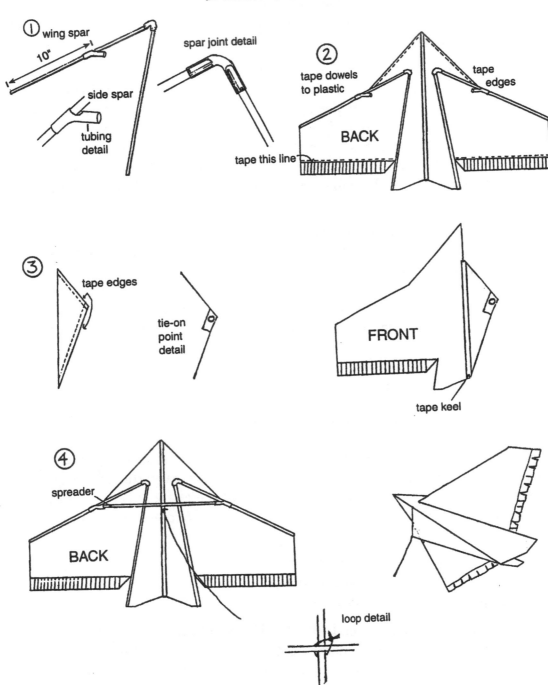

① wing spar

10"

side spar

tubing detail

spar joint detail

② tape dowels to plastic

tape edges

BACK

tape this line

③ tape edges

tie-on point detail

FRONT

tape keel

④ spreader

BACK

loop detail

Fabric Delta Kites

There are two ways of laying out and cutting a fabric delta kite–the one-piece and the two-piece. The one-piece has the center spar on the straight grain of the material and the leading edges off-grain. The two-piece typically has the leading edges on the grain and the center line off-grain.

Sailcloth is stable enough that this placement, as long as it is symmetrical, does not make that much difference. Two-piece construction uses material more economically; that is, two sets of wings can be cut from the same material that would yield a single one-piece delta. However, this is sans keels, and, if several one-piece are cut from a single length of material, they can be placed with the base first on one edge, then on the other, accomplishing the same economy. Certain piecing effects may dictate the choice; chevron stripes are easily accomplished with two-piece construction.

If one-piece wings are folded right sides together so the sleeve for the center spar is on the back, the fin keel can be inserted in the fold and stitched in place with one pass through the machine. This is also a neat possibility with the two-piece wing: first, a seam (wrong sides together) to join the wings. Fold the wings on the stitched edge, right sides together, raw edges inside. Sandwich the keel between the layers and stitch the sleeve seam, leaving an opening near the base for spar insertion.

Harper's Ferry Delta Kite

This kite was developed at a Maryland Kite Association retreat in Harpers Ferry, West Virginia, hence the name. I had demonstrated a poly bag delta and Mel Govig took the resulting kite as a pattern for a one-piece fabric delta, which Angela Dittmar and Alice Mackey stitched to go. Success depends on the lightweight crispness of coated spinnaker cloth. I have also scaled the Harper's Ferry Delta to 1 1/2 times the dimensions given here, and framed it with 3/16" dowels (drawing on right).

Materials: 1 1/2 yards .75 spinnaker cloth
1/8" dowels, two 14", two 17"
thread, and eyelet (optional)

Tools: hot knife, straight edge

1.   Fold the material end to end. Place "fold" edge of pattern on the fold with the long edge on the selvage. Cut out the kite with hot knife. Cut the fringe. I use the width of my yardstick as a guide. Mark the center spar line, the base line and the spreader points.

2.   Without opening the kite, stitch as shown, beginning 1/4" from the top and backstitching at beginning and end. This forms the keel and the sleeve for the spine. Open the kite, carefully separating the edges. A narrow blade, a letter opener, for example, is useful for separating edges which have been hot cut together.

3.   Make the spreader spar pockets as shown using scrap material or 1 1/2"-wide ribbon. Other spreader attachments may be used. (See Spreader Bar Options).

4.   On the back, turn 1/4" on the leading edges. Clip at the tip and stitch to form the sleeves, aligning the pockets and catching them in the seams as shown. Edge-stitch, because the sleeves are snug. Stitch across the lower ends.

5.   Insert an eyelet or loop of thread in the tip of the keel. Insert dowels: 14" in spine sleeve, 17" in side sleeves. The remaining 14" dowel is the spreader and may need to be adjusted for individual kites.

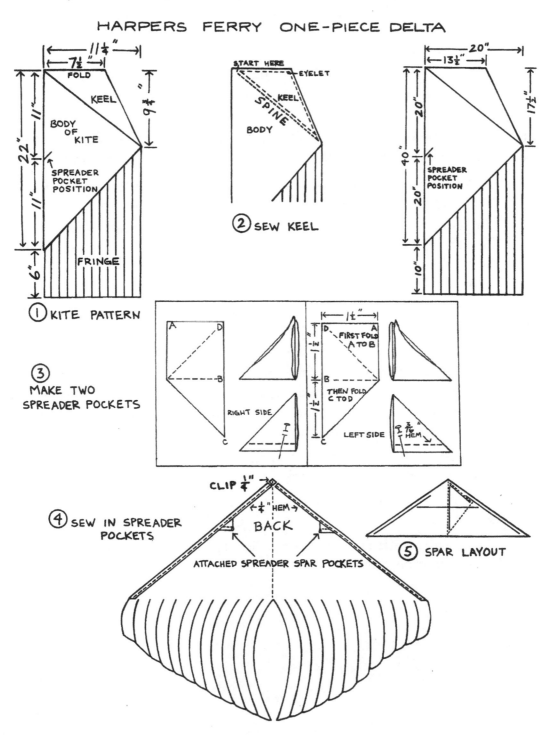

HARPERS FERRY ONE-PIECE DELTA

Zephyr Delta Kite

"One of the best-flying kites yet evolved," is the way Ed Grauel describes his Zephyr, a patented kite. The keel is a large, closed cell. If most deltas fly like butterflies, this one flies like a heavy-bodied moth. The closed cell gives stability in higher winds.

Materials: 2 yds. 40" material, kite made of one fabric or 1 2/3 yds. for kite,
      2/3 yd. for contrasting keel
a small amount of heavier material for reinforcements
three 3/16" dowels, one 33", two 28" long
one 1/4" dowel, about 35" long
fittings for spreader bar attachment
eyelet for tie-on

1.   Cut out the kite and transfer all markings to the fabric. Reinforce the lower tips of the leading edges and the top and bottom of the spine sleeve.

    Consider the options for attaching the spreader. If tape-and-ring, shown here, are used, stitch to the leading edges before closing the sleeves.

    Run a line of stitching along the sleeve fold lines of the leading (top) edges. Turn and press 1/4" to the wrong side of these edges. Turn and press again on the stitched fold line. Stitch across the bottom of the sleeve and up the sides to the top. Sleeves remain open at the top for spar insertion.

    Wrong sides together, fold the kite on the center line. Stitch 1/2" from the center line and across both ends of the sleeve. Break the stitching about 1" from the base and leave a 1" opening for inserting the spine.

    Narrowly hem the top edge of the keel. Turn the bottom and side edges under 1/4". Fold on the center line and stitch 1/2" from the folded edge, backstitching at both ends. Stitch the bottom edges together from the center to a point 3" from the outer edges. Reinforce the tie-on point and insert an eyelet.

2.   Matching the keel placement lines, pin or tape the keel in place, wrong side of keel to right side of kite. Stitch on the parallel marked lines.

    Insert the 28" dowels in the side sleeves, and the 33" dowel in the center sleeve.

3.   The spreader is sized to hold the kite flat. The length will vary. The spreader is inserted through the retainer loop.

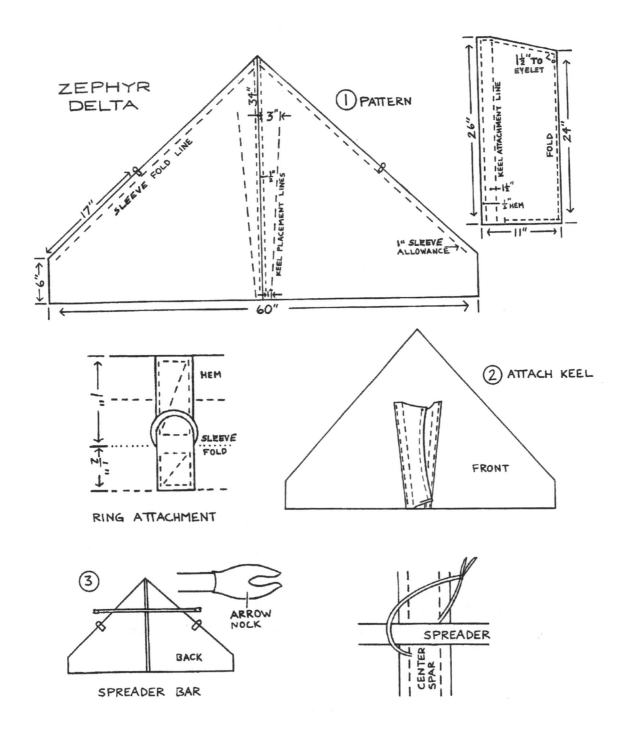

ZEPHYR
DELTA

① PATTERN

1½" TO
EYELET

26"

KEEL ATTACHMENT LINE

FOLD

24"

3¼"

3"

KEEL PLACEMENT LINES

SLEEVE FOLD LINE

17"

6"

1" SLEEVE
ALLOWANCE

60"

1¼"

½" HEM

11"

HEM

SLEEVE
FOLD

1"

2½"

RING ATTACHMENT

② ATTACH KEEL

FRONT

③

ARROW
NOCK

BACK

SPREADER BAR

SPREADER

CENTER
SPAR

Box Kites

I have been teaching kitemaking to teachers and students of all ages for over thirty years. I rarely come into a classroom without having someone ask if I ever make box kites. And I recognize the gleam in the eye of the questioner. My brother built a box kite when he was twelve and he talks about it still.

What a joy, then, to find the classic box in this version by Bill Lee of the Washington Kitefliers Association. It is not a fifteen-minute kite, and is too difficult for young students. Care and precision are needed, but you will be rewarded with an ultra-light two-cell box kite.

The tall kitchen trashbag can vary in size from brand to brand. The width of the bag determines the length of the spreaders. Multiply the width by .75 for the approximate spreader length. Expect to have to trim a bit. Look also for bags of somewhat heavier weight, up to 1 mil. Connectors are made of plastic tubing, inner diameter 1/8". Twist-ties are useful for tieing spreaders together and allow the kite to be disassembled and rolled for storage.

Cut a 4" paper template to facilitate marking the cutouts.

Bill Lee's Trashbag Box Kite Instructions

Materials: 1 tall kitchen trash bag (13 gal. size)
four 1/8" dia. 4' dowels, cut four 24" longerons and four spreaders
bridle string, 4 yards
3/4" cellophane tape
16" plastic tubing, cut in 2" lengths
two twist-ties

Tools: scissors, utility knife, marking pen, yardstick, snap clothespin

1.   Unfold the bag and slit open the bottom. Measure 24" from the top and trim the bag to this length. Fold the bag as shown. Snap clothespins will hold the folds together. Trace around the 4" template for the cutaways. Hold all thicknesses firmly together and cut out. Unfold. Two of the edges of the box will be the creases on the sides of the bag. Carefully measure and mark centers between these creases for the other edges.

2.   Mark 4" from both ends of the 24" longerons. This is the spreader location. Make a cut as shown in the middle of each tube. Slip tubes on the longerons and tape in place as shown. Insert the longerons in the bag, connectors facing the center, and tape to the bag over the ends and at the top, bottom and middle along the dowel. See sketch for taping the dowel ends.

3.   Cut the spreaders to the approximate length and insert in the connectors. They should bow outward slightly for good tension. Fasten each set of spreaders together with twist-ties.

4. Tie the ends of the bridle string all the way around the box at the spreaders. Set the tie-on point by holding the kite to the wind, or by choosing a point which suspends the kite at a 15 degree angle to the horizontal. If the kite flies to one side or the other, the bridle can be rotated to find the best flying edge. Or the top and bottom cells can be reversed. This wrap-around string also strengthens the kite for heavier winds. Tape the bridle to the kite when the optimum placement is found.

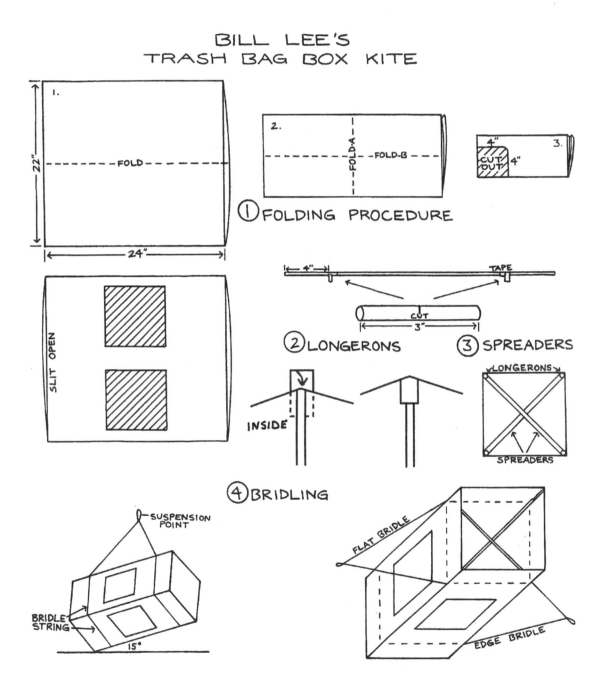

Mylar Mini Winged Box Kite

This little kite illustrates the technique for building box kites of mylar. One-half mil mylar is not stiff enough to maintain rigidity in a larger kite. The size could be increased if all edges are reinforced with cellophane tape. The vivid, transparent colors of mylar make gorgeous kites, but it is somewhat difficult to work with. Look for it in gift wrap displays.

Some tips: A white working surface is a help. I stacked the colors, drew around the patterns with a marker and cut several pieces at once. Use scissors or a sharp knife. Mylar becomes electrically charged and grabs for the tape. The flat-on-the-table fin-cell assembly worked best.

Materials: 1/2 mil mylar in multi-colors
three 1/8" dia. dowels, 3' long
strapping tape
16" bridle string

1.   Make the pattern and cut out the kite.

2.   Tape the longerons to the cells as shown.

3.   Bring the free edges of the cells together and join with tape. Butt together and tape both sides.

4.   Reinforce the fin tips and punch holes as shown.

5.   Be sure all the fins head the same way as you tape them to the longerons. Begin by lining up one of each. Lay a piece of tape on the fin, across and around the stick to the other side of the fin. When you are finished with the first fin, give the cell a quarter turn to do the next.

6.   Spreader spars, approximately 13 1/2" long, are notched at the ends to slip into the holes on the fin tips.

7.   Bridle with needle and thread as shown.

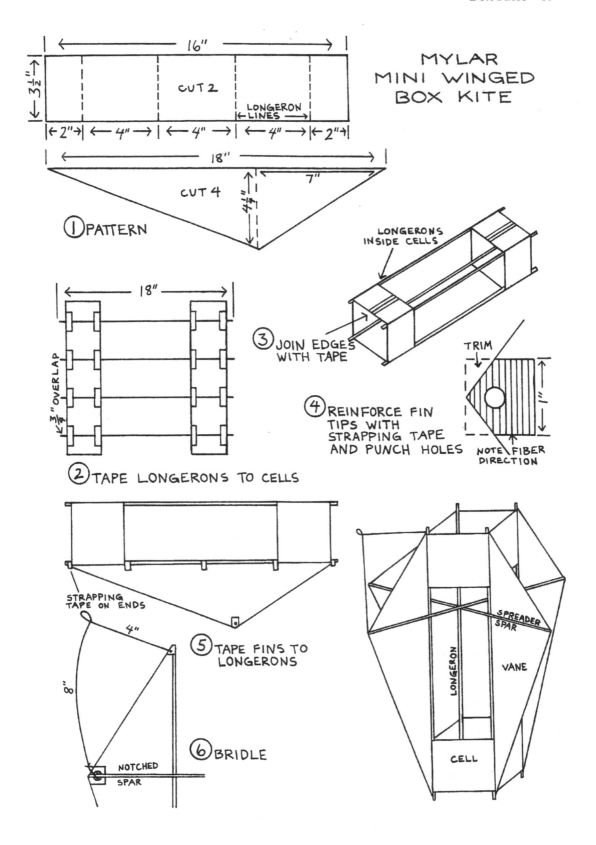

MYLAR
MINI WINGED
BOX KITE

16"

3½"

CUT 2

LONGERON
LINES

←2"→ ←4"→ ←4"→ ←4"→ ←2"→

① PATTERN

18"

CUT 4

4¼"

7"

LONGERONS
INSIDE CELLS

③ JOIN EDGES
WITH TAPE

TRIM

1"

NOTE FIBER
DIRECTION

④ REINFORCE FIN
TIPS WITH
STRAPPING TAPE
AND PUNCH HOLES

18"

¾" OVERLAP

② TAPE LONGERONS TO CELLS

STRAPPING
TAPE ON ENDS

4"

⑤ TAPE FINS TO
LONGERONS

8"

⑥ BRIDLE

NOTCHED
SPAR

SPREADER
SPAR

LONGERON

VANE

CELL

Fabric Box Kite

Invented by Lawrence Hargraves of Australia in 1893, the box kite swept the scientific world. It was a breakthrough when the major inventors of the time had their heads full of schemes for flying machines. During the late 1800s through the early 1900s, scores of variations on boxes and boxes-with-wings were built and tested, many with a view to harnessing the lifting power of these kites. In the days before Kitty Hawk, the weather services and the military of many Western countries had what might be called fleets of kites which were used for observation. Big kites to begin with, they were flown in train to lift instruments, bulky cameras, even observers. Hargraves did not patent his work. Believing that such discoveries could advance civilization, he presented all his findings to the world through scientific papers.

The Conyne Kite, also known as the French Military, was patented by an American, Silas Conyne, in 1902. It is a compound kite, combining cells with plane surfaces.

New materials have simplified the construction of the Winged Square Box. The Corner and the Facet are modern boxes, designs of our time, also inspiring many variations. The Corner was first patented by Francis Rogallo as a radar reflector, another working kite.

Fabric Box Kite Tips

Because boxes are usually made of multi-colors, calculation of fabric requirements is left to the kitemaker. The patterns are given without hem allowances, with edge binding assumed. If hems are preferred, make allowance.

Lay all pattern pieces on the straight of the fabric, either with or across the grain.

It is important to reinforce the ends of the sleeves. Spar tips can also be cushioned with plastic end caps sold for the purpose.

Box kites fly well only when they are precisely constructed and the vanes and cells are tightly stretched. Measure, mark and stitch with care. Floppy, flabby vanes and cells mean a poor flyer.

French Military Kite Instructions

Materials: fabric, dimensions from pattern
five 1/4" dowels, 4' long
45" of 80# test line
five 1/2" dia. split rings
9 yards ribbon for binding and sleeves
4 arrow nocks 1/4" inner diameter

Follow the instructions for the Winged Square Box. Positioning of the ring-and-tape for the lower spreader is best done after joining the cells and fins.

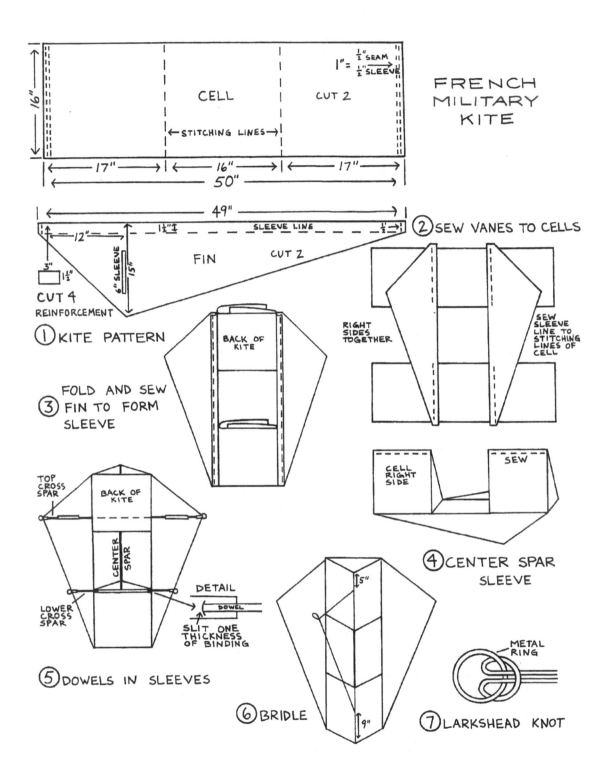

Winged Square Box Kite

The simplified construction of this classic means that if you have faith and follow the instructions a step at a time, when you turn things right side out you will have an elegant box kite, ready to fly in almost any wind. I used spinnaker sailcloth and it flies in barely 5 mph.

Materials: sailcloth, dimensions from pattern
six 1/4" diameter 4' dowels
12 yards tape for edge binding
80# fishline for bridle
nine 1/2" diameter rings
material for reinforcements
4 arrow nocks, 1/4" inner diameter

1. Cut out. Mark all stitching lines.

2. Sew reinforcements at the ends of the sleeves so the spars won't poke through. Bind the long edges of the cells and the off-grain edges of the fins, mitering the binding at the corner so the fabric stays flat.

3. Make ring-and-tape attachments and sew them to the fin tips.

4. Sew the fins to the cells, backstitching all seams.

5. Turn under one-fourth inch on the long edges of the sleeves, turn again, bringing the folded edge to match the stitching line which joins the vane to the cell. Sew the whole length of the sleeves and across both ends, except for backstitching and leaving a 1" opening about 1" up from the bottom edge for spar insertion. The spar sleeve stands away from the kite, instead of being sewed flat to it.

6. Lay the kite flat, fins up. Keeping fins inside, bring free edges of the cells together, stitching as shown. Press to one side and edgestitch the seam flat to the cell. Turn the cells right side out. Fit the longerons into the sleeves.

7. The spreader length can vary, depending on the precision of construction and the method of spar attachment. It will be approximately 38 1/2" plus arrow nocks. Line the nocks up so the slots are in the same plane. The spreaders should square the cells and stretch the fins taut. After they are in place, rings may be sewed to the sleeves at the juncture with the spreaders (detail). Slipping the spreaders through the rings strengthens the kite.

8. Box kites are bridled to be edge-flown or flat-flown. If you want to compare the options, you can rig a quick bridle with line attached by safety pins to the firmly-bound edges. Use 80# test line, about 30" for the edge-flown and 6' for the flat. Thread the line in a needle, run it through the edge binding and tie it around the longeron. Through the binding at the front tip of the fin will do for the edge-flown.

WINGED SQUARE BOX KITE

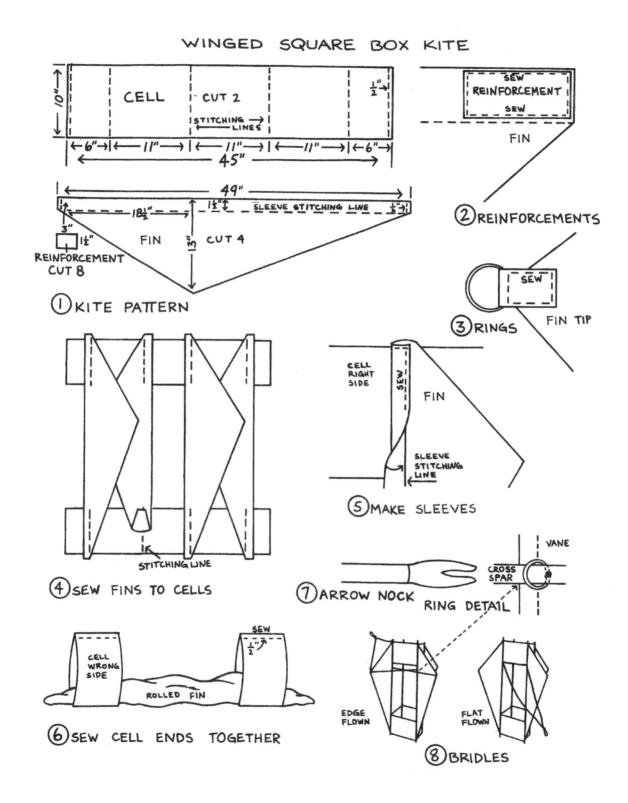

10"

CELL   CUT 2

½"

STITCHING
LINES →

←6"→ ← 11" → ← 11" → ← 11" → ←6"→
45"

SEW
REINFORCEMENT
SEW

FIN

② REINFORCEMENTS

49"

1¼"   SLEEVE STITCHING LINE   ½"

18½"

3"
1¼"
REINFORCEMENT
CUT 8

FIN   13"   CUT 4

① KITE PATTERN

SEW

FIN TIP

③ RINGS

CELL
RIGHT
SIDE   SEW   FIN

SLEEVE
STITCHING
LINE

⑤ MAKE SLEEVES

STITCHING LINE

④ SEW FINS TO CELLS

VANE

CROSS
SPAR

⑦ ARROW NOCK   RING DETAIL

SEW
½"

CELL
WRONG
SIDE   ROLLED FIN

⑥ SEW CELL ENDS TOGETHER

EDGE
FLOWN

FLAT
FLOWN

⑧ BRIDLES

Rogallo Corner Kite

The Corner Kite, patented by Francis Rogallo as a radar reflector, is used here with Rogallo's permission. It is a box kite, a stable flier which loves the wind. After Lawrence Hargraves invented the box kite and gave it to the world in 1893, other inventors began playing with the possibilities of the flying enclosed space, and almost every imaginable solid configuration–cubes, rectangles, prisms, pyramids and cylinders–was tried, many of them by Hargraves. The Corner Kite turns the box inside out, forming a cube with interior corners. With its intersecting vanes, it is particularly easy to make in fabric and the plain/plane surfaces call for the imaginative use of color.

Single-Cell Corner Kite Instructions

Materials: two 33" squares of sailcloth
one 5/16" dowel, 4' long
four 1/4" dowels
five 1/2" dia. split rings
20" of 1/2" or 5/8" poly ribbon
16" plastic tubing, inside dia. 1/4"
material for reinforcements

1. The squares may be hemmed or bound. Since the edges are all on-grain, I usually hem. Draw around the square pattern on the fabric and add 1/2" hem allowance. Lay a straight edge from one corner to another and draw the diagonal on each square. To hem, stitch on the fold lines, then turn the edge twice and stitch the hems.

    Reinforce at both ends of the diagonals as shown for the Winged Square Box. Line up the squares, matching and pinning the center lines. Stitch 3/8" on each side of the center and across the ends, forming a sleeve. Leave a 1" opening near the lower edge for spar insertion. (See the Facet Kite for an alternative method for the center spar.)

2. Double the ribbon lengthwise and stitch to make tape for the connectors. Cut it in 4" lengths and stitch to each outside corner as shown. Insert rings. Cut the tubing in 4" lengths, and thread four of the rings through the centers of the tubing. Cut the center spar to size and insert.

    Tubing connectors: I use an icepick to make the holes in the tubing and needlenosed pliers to spread the ring and work it through the holes. The holes can also be drilled.

    The tubing connectors make spreader adjustment easier. Theoretically, a spreader for a kite made of 33" equilateral triangles should be 33", but this does vary. Start with sticks at least one inch longer and trim as needed. (If too much is cut off, a whole set of spars will have to be put aside for a smaller kite.)

If the spreaders are made just slightly longer than the distance to be spanned they will bow and put tension on the vanes. Taper the spreader tips slightly for easier insertion. Good tension is essential.

Bridle: The One-Cell Corner can be edge-flown or flat-flown, with a two-leg or a three-leg bridle. Use a ring and a larkshead knot for easy adjustment. Sew a ring at the top for the bridle and tie the lower ends through the connector rings.

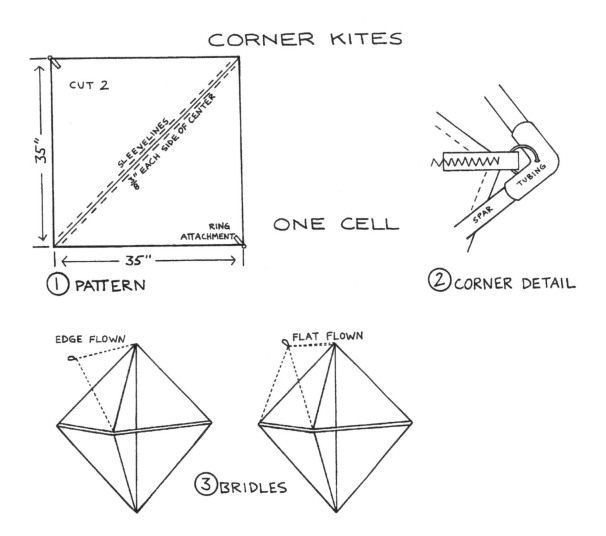

CORNER KITES

CUT 2

SLEEVELINES
3/8" EACH SIDE OF CENTER

35"

RING ATTACHMENT

35"

① PATTERN

ONE CELL

SPAR

TUBING

② CORNER DETAIL

EDGE FLOWN

FLAT FLOWN

③ BRIDLES

Two-Cell Corner Kite

Materials: four 24" squares of sailcloth (includes hem allowance)
67" fiberglass longeron, or two 3/8" dia. dowels, 33 1/2" each + metal
    tubing to ferrule them together
four 1/4" dia. dowels, 4' long
ten 1/2" dia. split rings
1 1/8 yards 1/2" wide ribbon for connectors
34" plastic tubing, 1/4" interior diameter
30# test line for guy lines
material for reinforcements

4.   Make cells as in the One-Cell Corner. Stitch connector loops at each outer
corner. A small ring or a loop of tape, for tieing the cells together, is sewn at
the open tip of the center sleeve of each cell.

    I use a fiberglass rod for the longeron. If you are using dowels, connect them
with a 4"-long metal tubing sleeve or ferrule.

    Two-Cell Assembly: Insert the longerons in the sleeves. Tie the cells together
as shown. Begin with 24" spreaders and trim as needed.

5.   Guy lines from an upper corner to two lower corners and from a lower corner
to two upper corners, four lines altogether, hold the two cells in alignment
when flying. I knot the line at the centers and adjust at the ends.

    Tie to any corner to fly. To disassemble, remove the spreaders, laying the vanes
flat on each other. Lightly roll the vanes around the center spar for bagging.
Assemble in the same way, rolling the structure as the spreaders are inserted,
one cell and then the next, to avoid tangling the guy lines.

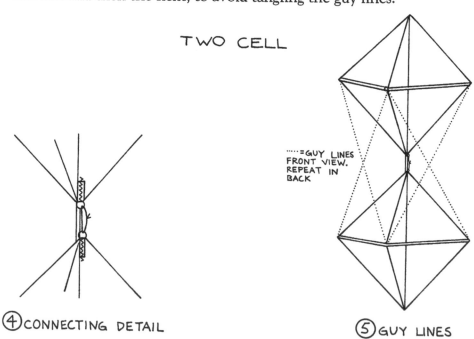

TWO CELL

·····=GUY LINES
FRONT VIEW.
REPEAT IN
BACK

④ CONNECTING DETAIL   ⑤ GUY LINES

Facet Kites

Stephen Robinson of England developed the Facets and his designs were first published in *Kite Lines* magazine. We are all in his debt. Robinson says the Facet is a "tensegrity" structure, with the rods in compression and the material in tension. The easy, logically-satisfying construction produces a three-dimensional honeycomb. Facets can be addictive as they bloom in the sky in endless color combinations. They fly well in light-to-medium winds and, with their chandelier-like shapes, decorate interior space as well.

Facet possibilities are being explored by kitemakers around the world. There are Facet tetrahedrons, cubes, pentahedrons, and hexahedrons. Remember that more cells may add weight without a corresponding gain in lifting surface.

When I began work on the Facet, I made a tissue paper version, using 6", 4", and 2" squares and three colors. The pieces were joined by running the folded edge of each segment over the top of a gluestick. Construction paper and staples can also be used to work out color combinations and schemes for weaving the panels.

The twelve-inch, four-sided Facet shown here has two cell "steps", in this case formed of 12", 8" and 4" squares, joined on the diagonals. It scales directly and quite large Facets have been made and flown. The five-sided Facet has a one-step cell structure and the two kites illustrate the principles of Facet Kite construction. Kitebuilders can adapt them to other configurations.

Because the small Facet is heavy for its lifting surface it needs a medium wind and a tail for stability. The little Facets can be flown in train without tails, branching off the line as shown for the Dutch Kite. Two cells may be joined on a single center spar, as for the two-cell Corner, with the tie-on on any corner.

A six-sided Facet sized to the width of the material, with two-step cells, has a 51" diagonal, and fills a small room. Graphite or fiberglass spars are essential on the larger Facets because dowels will warp in time and are not stiff enough for good tension. On the larger Facets, it is easier to tension a five- or six-sided kite than a four-sided. Scott Spencer, a New Jersey Facet maker, flies at the beach, and carries a set of slightly longer spars to re-tension his kite when the fabric stretches from dampness. Fabric also stretches with age and use.

Twelve-inch Four-sided Facet Kite (starter Facet)

Materials: two 12" squares, four 8" squares, four 4" squares of .75 oz sailcloth
four 1/8" dowels, about 12" long
one 1/8" dowel, about 16 1/2" long
8" plastic tubing, 1/8" inner diameter
4 small rings (optional)
needle, button thread
material for reinforcements

1. Cut the squares with a hot knife. Make a 12" pattern with heavy black diagonal lines and lay the squares on this one by one, smaller squares lined up with the corners, to trace the diagonals.

2. Sew the large squares together, stitching 1/8" on each side of the center diagonal and across the ends for a sleeve. Leave an opening for spar insertion. Assemble two sets of medium and small squares. Pair the mediums and sew together as shown. Open the pair and, with the points up and the small squares underneath, sew a small square to each outside corner as shown.

   Matching corners, sew the long diagonals of the medium squares to the large squares, one set on the front and one on the back, carefully pulling the large squares away so the stitching is through two layers only. Lastly, sew the tips of the large squares together on the short diagonals. Insert the center spar.

3. There are twenty "wing tips" on the outer perimeter of the kite. Reinforce all the tips. A small triangle of adhesive material will do. The center point of each group of three is a corner, four in all. Leave the corners free and bring the outside tips together in pairs, two pairs to a side. Join by sewing a small ring to each pair.

   Option: Sew the pairs together with button thread. Then make a loop large enough for the dowel to pass through. Secure the loop with a couple of stitches.

4-5. Cut the tubing into four 2" lengths. Push a needle through the middle and sew the tubing to the corners somewhat loosely, so it can twist to accommodate the spars. Slip the dowels through the rings on each side before forcefitting into the tubing.

6. Bridle as shown.

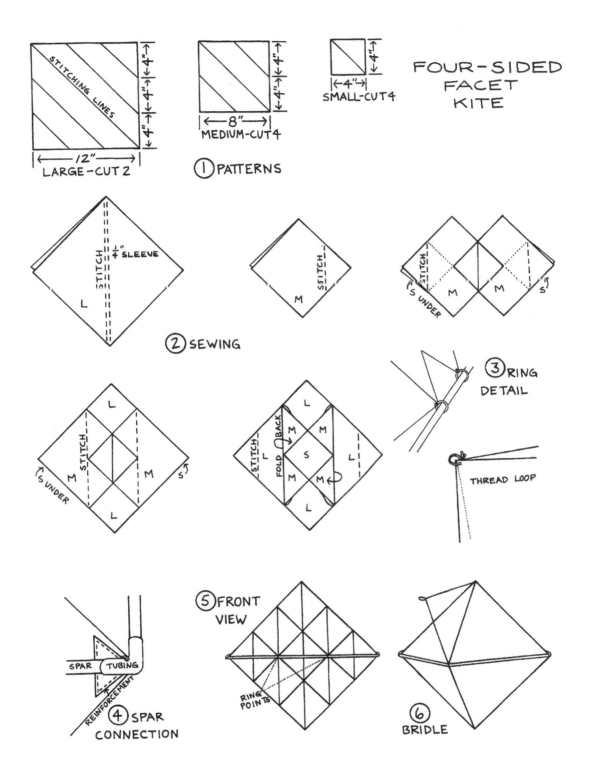

STITCHING LINES

←— 12" —→
LARGE—CUT 2

↓ 4" ↓ 4" ↓ 4" ↓

←— 8" —→
MEDIUM—CUT4

↓ 4" ↓ 4" ↓

←4"→
SMALL-CUT4

↓ 4" ↓

FOUR–SIDED
FACET
KITE

① PATTERNS

STITCH   ↓ 1/4" SLEEVE
L

② SEWING

M   STITCH

STITCH   ↑ S UNDER   M   M   S ↗

L   L
M   STITCH   M
M   M
L   L
↑ S UNDER   S ↗

L   L
FOLD BACK
STITCH   M   M
L   S   L
M   M
L   L

③ RING
DETAIL

THREAD LOOP

SPAR   TUBING
REINFORCEMENT
④ SPAR
CONNECTION

⑤ FRONT
VIEW

RING
POINTS

⑥
BRIDLE

Five-Sided (Star) Facet Kite

Both Stephen Robinson and Scott Spencer shared their Facetmaking techniques. The bead-and-arrow-nock tensioning was developed by Scott Spencer and could be used on other box kites. Many of the other details were worked out by Spencer. Various color patterns are possible, depending on how the small and large squares are sequenced. Make a paper mock-up first.

Stephen Robinson's method of hemming Facet squares: an ingenious way of forming the corners and inserting loops for the rings. Attaching the tape or cord in a V at the tips puts the tension on the hemmed edges. (Diagram #8)

Mark the squares and cut them with a 3/4" seam allowance. Mark the diagonals. Fold and crease the corners as shown. Fold the edge of the seam allowance to the marked line and stitch all around, including the double-folded corners. Turn the edges on the fold line and stitch, including a 4" length of cord in opposite corners as shown. This can all be done in a single run of stitching with no breaks.

When the points are gathered for the insertion of the rings, the paired points on a side are joined with a wide zigzag bartack. The ring goes through both loops.

Using smaller rings for the sides than for the corners causes the spreaders to bow slightly, increasing tension.

The facet variation drawings are by Stephen Robinson.

Materials:
- two 24" fabric squares plus one 24" triangle
- five 12" squares
- center spar, 3/8" dia., approx. 36" long
- five spreaders, 1/4" dia., approx. 21" long
- split rings: five large enough for spreaders to pass through and five next size larger for the corners
- 15" plastic tubing, 1/4" inner dia., cut in 3" lengths
- 1 yard 1/2" ribbon, 2 1/2" of 1" ribbon
- two arrow nocks large enough to accommodate the center spar (taper the ends with a pencil sharpener)
- four round wooden beads with holes large enough for 80# line to pass through
- approx. 4 yards of 80-100# test line

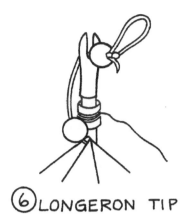

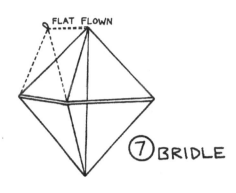

⑥LONGERON TIP

⑦BRIDLE

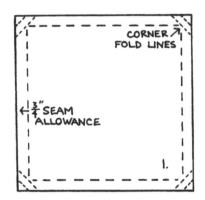

CORNER
FOLD LINES

←$\frac{3}{4}$" SEAM
ALLOWANCE

1.

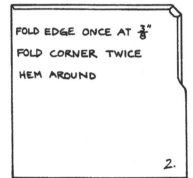

FOLD EDGE ONCE AT $\frac{3}{8}$"

FOLD CORNER TWICE

HEM AROUND

2.

HEMMING SQUARES

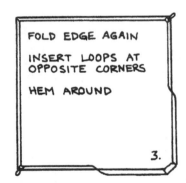

FOLD EDGE AGAIN

INSERT LOOPS AT
OPPOSITE CORNERS

HEM AROUND

3.

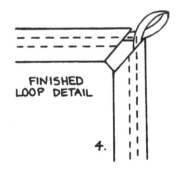

FINISHED
LOOP DETAIL

4.

FACET VARIATIONS

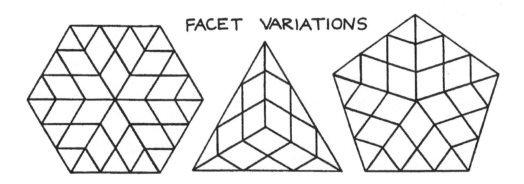

1. Cut patterns the size of the finished squares and draw around them to outline the hemline. Add 1/2" on all sides when cutting. Cut the triangle as shown. Mark diagonals on each piece, from corner to corner of the square. Hem the squares and the outer edges of the triangle.

2. The triangle is sandwiched between the squares and it is easier to do this if the triangle and one square are stitched together first. Include a loop for the center spar (2 1/2" of 1"-wide ribbon) in the seam as shown. Carefully match the diagonals and stitch the second large square to the square/triangle assembly. Use a long stitch with a very narrow zigzag.

3. Match the small squares to the corners and stitch on the diagonals.

4. There are now five sets with three points each. The center point is the corner and the outer two are pulled left and right to join with the matching point from the nearest corner. Form loops with 2" lengths of ribbon. Stitch one on each corner and pair of points as shown.

5. Insert the smaller rings in the tape loops of the paired points (sides of kite.) Insert the larger rings in tubing and the ring-and-tube in the corner loops.

6. Taper the ends of the longeron. Two narrow (about 1/8") washers cut from plastic tubing can be slipped over one end to form a bridle stay. Glue the arrow nocks on the longeron tips. Make the bead and loop assembly as shown on p. 101.

   The spreader length can vary. Cut the spreaders 1/2" longer than the projected length and work from there. Insert four spreaders. The overage on the fifth will help you calculate how much should be trimmed from each one.

7. Three-point bridle: (See Corner Kite, p. 95) Cut 10' of line. Find the center and tie the line between the plastic washers on the longeron. Tie the ends through two adjacent corner rings. Bring the two large loops thus formed together with a ring-and-larkshead-knot. The top leg of the bridle should be at an angle a little less than perpendicular to the longeron.

   Facets fly in somewhat lighter winds and at a higher angle with a three-leg bridle. Testing various bridles is simple since the rings serve as tie-ons and the many faces permit a two-leg on one side of the kite and a three-leg on another for easy comparison. The size of the kite and the wind in which it is flown will determine the best bridling method.

   When removing the spars from the tubing connectors, pushing works better than pulling, which only serves to tighten the tube on the wood. George Ham uses a pusher, a short length of wood with a notch which fits over the spar. A spring clothespin works well on small diameter spreaders.

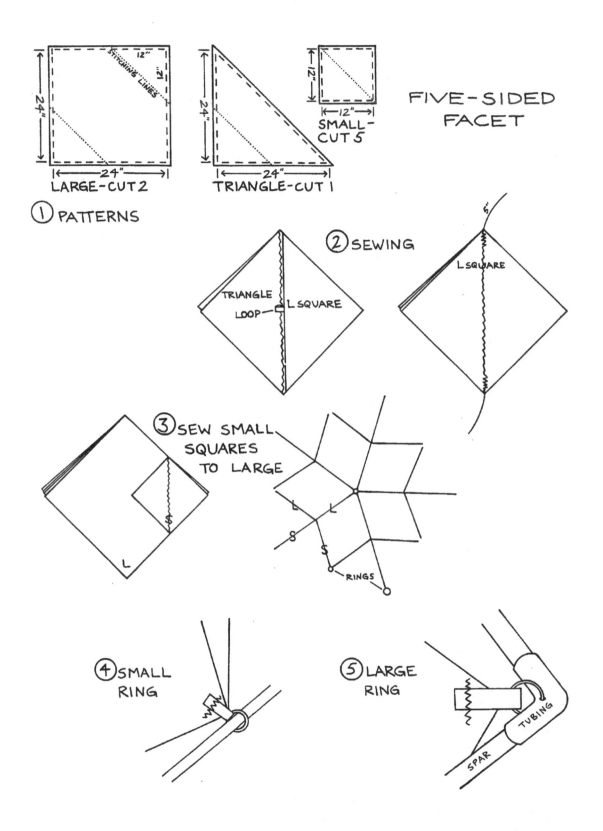

FIVE-SIDED FACET

① PATTERNS

② SEWING

③ SEW SMALL SQUARES TO LARGE

④ SMALL RING

⑤ LARGE RING

Flow Form Kite

Invented by Domina Jalbert in the sixties, the parafoil kite was something new in the sky. Jalbert called it "the most powerful lifting device in the world for its weight and pack-volume when flown within its operational limits." There are no bones in parafoils. The wind fills the air-mattress-like cells and the shape of the kite is maintained by internal pressure and by multiple bridle (shroud) lines. The present day parachute is a parafoil structure, as is the paraglider, a "soft" hang glider.

The Flow Form, developed and patented by Steve Sutton of Toronto, is easy to make, to bridle and to handle, a "poor woman's parafoil." Bridled at the top only, like a sled, the pull is relatively light. The Flow Form Kite looks like a pair of trousers, a clown or a giant molar. The legs may be elongated and tapered. Flow Forms have been scaled to large sizes, notably by Art Ross of Vancouver, Canada, and Don Mock of Seattle.

Making the Pattern and Cutting out the Kite

For easier construction, our pattern has been somewhat modified from the original. For an accurate stitching line, draw around the pattern on the fabric and add 1/2" seam allowances as shown in the pattern diagrams. The easy way to finish outer edges and add bridle loops is to bind with grosgrain ribbon. Since all edges are hemmed, bound or inside, hot cutting is not necessary except for the vents. Make the vent template with holes. It's easier to hot cut a hole than to cut around a circle.

This pattern simplifies construction by joining the center fin to the left front and the inner rib to the right front. Remember to lay all pattern pieces on the straight of the material.

Use .75 oz. spinnaker cloth. The crisp, lightweight fabric makes it easy for the cells to open and fill. Most parafoils are multi-colored and the amount of fabric needed can be calculated from the layout. White material for the back will intensify bright colors on the front. The Flow Form takes about five yards of 41" width sailcloth. Since sailcloth comes in several widths, the yardage will vary.

The top of the pattern in the diagram is the leading edge, the bottom the trailing edge. Put another way, the top of the pattern piece in the layout will be at the top of the finished kite. Mark the top edges with pins or chalk. It will also help to keep things straight if you designate a "wrong" side and put seam and stitching markings on it. Dotted lines in the pattern are stitching lines or show a second layer underneath.

After the kite is cut out, mark the stitching lines on the rib/fins and front panels. Mark on the wrong side and use a #2 pencil or a marker so the lines show. The vents are 2" in diameter and spacing is from the top edge of the kite to the center of the hole. Hot cut vents in three inner ribs and in the front panel.

Polyester thread is recommended. Use a #14 or #16 (jeans) needle and change as needed. Backstitch all seams and binding. Stitch wide to narrow, top to bottom. Use tape or Dry-Line to hold the pieces together for stitching.

Binding: Start with a full bobbin. Use a long stitch when binding. If you have a folder/binder attachment for your machine, give it a practice try. It can make binding easy and fun. Chain where practical. Chaining means binding one piece after another without cutting the tape or the thread in between. If the chain gets too long, clip the pieces apart as you go. When you stop binding, keep stitching for a couple of inches before cutting the tape, leaving a tag hanging out and the folder ready for the next piece. Cut ends can be sealed with Fray-Check.

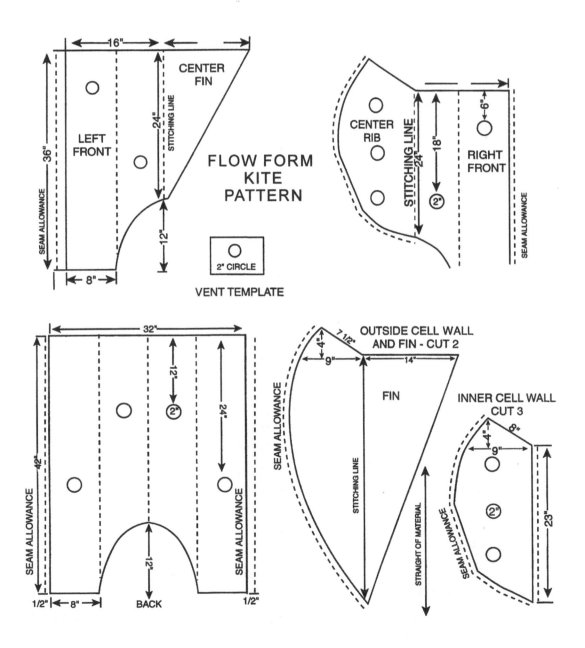

Flow Form Kite Instructions

Materials: .75 oz spinnaker sailcloth
about 9 yards 1/2" or 5/8" ribbon
10 yards 80# test braided line
Fray-Check
double-sided sewing tape or Dry-Line for joining seams
before stitching

Bind: top edge and curved bottom edge of the front
curved bottom edge of the back
leading edges of the side fins (forming loops at the bottom for tails,
if desired)
leading edge of the center fin/left front top piece, forming a bridle loop at the
tip of the fin
top edges of the inner ribs

1.   Lay the back face down. Starting at the top and matching curved edges to straight edges, join the side rib/fins to the back. Run tape or Dry Line along the edge of the back and place the rib edge on top for a lapped seam. Stitch from top to bottom on both edges of the seam.

   Bind the leading edge of this assembly, leaving a 3 1/2" tag on both fin tips. Fold the tags over and zigzag stitch the bridle loops. Lay the back aside and pick up the two front pieces.

2.   Place the left front /fin on the table wrong side up. Top with the right front/ center rib, wrong side up and stitching lines matched. Join with a straight stitch, backstitching at both ends. Turn assembly over.

3.   Sew the straight edges of the inner ribs to the wrong side of the front, matching the stitching lines on the front to the seam lines on the ribs and backstitching top and bottom. Roll the kite to fit under the head of the machine.

4.   Turn under and press towards the wrong side a 1/2" seam allowance on both raw edges of the kite front. Lay the back/side assembly wrong side up. Wrong sides together, match the left turned-under edge of the front to the stitching line on the left rib/fin. Topstitch.

5.   Lay the back of the kite inner side up on the table. One at a time, beginning at the left, match the curved edges of the three ribs, including the center rib, to the stitching lines on the back. Secure with tape and stitch. Seam edges face right.

   Wrong sides together, match the right turned edge to the stitching line on the right rib/fin. Topstitch and backstitch.

6.   At the base of the kite, pin and stitch the free edges of the front and back together across the bottom and into the arch, leaving a 6" opening, 3" on each side of the center line.

FLOW FORM KITE

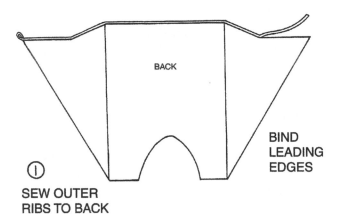

BACK

① SEW OUTER
RIBS TO BACK

BIND
LEADING
EDGES

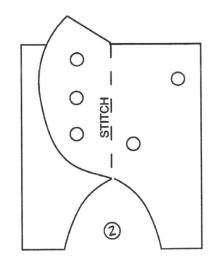

STITCH

②

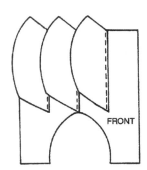

FRONT

③ SEW STRAIGHT EDGES
OF RIBS TO FRONT

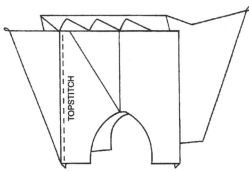

TOPSTITCH

④ TOPSTITCH FRONT LEFT
SIDE TO OUTSIDE FIN

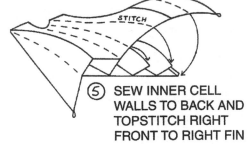

STITCH

⑤ SEW INNER CELL
WALLS TO BACK AND
TOPSTITCH RIGHT
FRONT TO RIGHT FIN

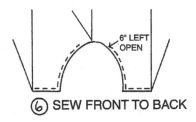

6" LEFT
OPEN

⑥ SEW FRONT TO BACK

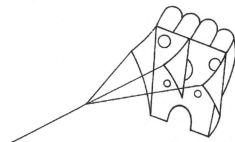

Bridling and Flying the Flow Form

Cut one 20' and one 10' piece of line. Tie the ends of the 20' line into the loops on the outer fins and one end of the 10' line into the loop on the center fin. Bring the fin tips together, matching the outer fin tips and pulling the center tip forward about 2". This gives the kite a slight dihedral. Call on a helper to hold the fin tips. Pull the lines together out to the ends and tie all three together with an overhand loop.

The flying line ties through this loop. Lines can stretch and knots can slip. If the kite should dive or fly erratically, check the the bridle and the fin alignment. The bridle may seem long to the point of being a nuisance, but experts say there's no such thing as too long. I loop the bridle over my hand as I bring it in and put a rubber band around it. Chaining, as in single crochet, is another option.

The Flow Form flies best in 5-15 mph winds. A drogue or tails can be added to increase the range. If the wind is right, launching is easy. Back to the wind, hold the reel in one hand with about ten feet of line out. Hold the bridle lines about three feet from the kite in the other hand. As the wind catches and fills the kite, release the lines and begin giving line from the reel. If a shoulder is crumpled, shaking the bridle will permit the wind to straighten it.

Kite Tails, Bags, and Windsocks

Tails

Tails are decorative as well as utilitarian. Paper and fabric strips can be grouped into tassels and ponytails. The continuous-loop tail could be made of a paper chain. Shape or fringe the ends of tails and streamers. Tube and banner tails made on a large scale are usually flown from one of the workhorse kites, a big box or a parafoil.

Drogue construction is shown in the diagram. This is a minimum size. Tangling of the harness is minimized if the lines are just long enough to allow the tube to open fully. A lead line with swivels at both ends attaches it to the kite. If the kite has a central panel (sled or delta) use a two-point attachment.

The tube tail should be lightweight. Spinnaker sailcloth is recommended. This tube, designed by Ed Grauel, has a 6"-wide strip of fabric joined to an 8"-wide strip. The last foot of the tube is tapered to a 1" diameter opening. Trim the 6" section of the top in a semi-circle and stiffen by binding. Sew 1/2"-wide velcro to the back of the 8" strip and at the lower edge of the kite.

The pieced banner tail is made of random widths of many colors, all cut 12" wide and pieced to the desired length, cut corner to corner, and the straight edges joined to make a tapered tail. Black and white accent and intensify the colors. If the fabric is hot-cut, hemming the edges is not necessary, though, particularly on long tails, hemming helps eliminate twisting. Long tails may need battens (See Fabric Snake.)

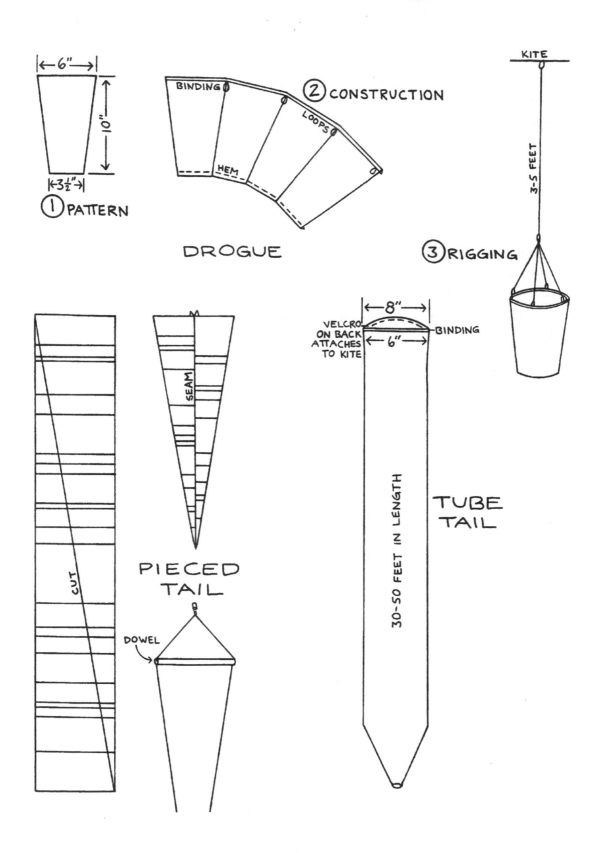

← 6" →

10"

|← 3½" →|

① PATTERN

BINDING

② CONSTRUCTION

LOOPS

HEM

DROGUE

③ RIGGING

KITE

3-5 FEET

CUT

SEAM

PIECED TAIL

DOWEL

VELCRO ON BACK ATTACHES TO KITE

← 8" →

BINDING

← 6" →

30-50 FEET IN LENGTH

TUBE TAIL

Kite Bags

A strip of fabric 7" wide and 4 1/2" longer than the longest dimension of the rolled kite will make a drawstring bag for most loosely-rolled delta and sled kites. The Facets and Corners, with their tubing connectors, need a 10" width. Nylon cord and shoelaces both make good drawstrings.

There is a school of bagmaking which finds satisfaction in packing a kite in the smallest possible bag. To my mind, this means more wrinkles and more wear and tear on the kite. A Flowform can be stuffed into a 5"x8" bag, but I prefer a 10"x16".

Diagrams 1-4 show how to make a good bag for a small soft kite. It is closed with an ingenious foldover. To calculate the size, measure the folded kite. Double the length measurement and add 4" for hems and foldovers. Add 1" to the width. The ends are finished as shown before the long sides are sewed together.

Diagrams 5-8 show a bag for a sparred kite. Make the bag the length of the kite plus 2". Measure the rolled kite for the width and add 3" for seams and an easy fit. The sewing sequence is: Fold the bag the long way, right sides together. Stitch across one end and up the side, stopping the stitching and backstitching 4" from the top edge. Hem the edges of the 4" opening by turning and stitching. Make the casing and insert a drawstring.

Instead of a drawstring, both ends of the bag can be closed with a 3"-4" opening left in the side seam next to the top for inserting the kite.

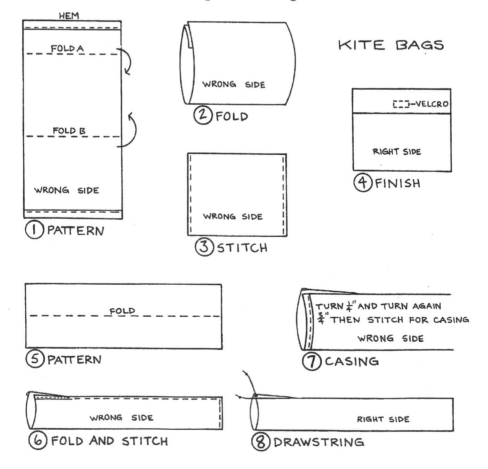

Streamer Windsock

This is a good craft project for camp or classroom. Surveyor's tape could be used for the streamers. Plastic tubing in many sizes comes from the hardware store. Make a handsome indoor windsock with ribbon or tissue paper streamers. Or hot cut sailcloth strips.

Materials: 19" plastic tubing, 1/4" inner diameter
2" of 1/4" dowel for joiner
30" braided line
medium-size snap swivel
8 plastic streamers, 2"x4'
tape

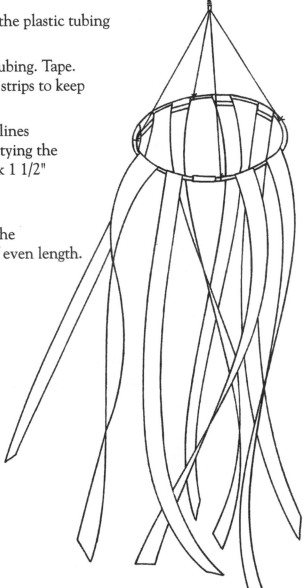

1.   Make a circle by joining the ends of the plastic tubing with the dowel.

2.   Fold one end of each strip over the tubing. Tape. You may also need tape between the strips to keep them in place.

3.   Cut two 15" pieces of line. Put both lines through the loop of the snap swivel, tying the swivel in the center of the line. Mark 1 1/2" from the ends of all the lines.

4.   Tie the lines to the frame, two strips between each pair of lines, holding the knot at the marks, so the lines are of even length.

MARK KNOT PLACEMENT

Ribbon Windsock

I begin with two yards each of six colors of ribbon for the tube and six yards each for streamers and make these little windsocks up by the batch, using them as small gifts for babies, anniversaries and graduations. Reading from the top, rainbows are red, orange, yellow, green, blue and violet.

Material for three windsocks: 1' each, six colors of 3/8" wide satin ribbon
1 yard each, six colors 1/4" satin ribbon
medium weight fusible interfacing, 1' x 1 1/2"
thread for harness

1. Lay the interfacing on the ironing board fusible side up. Line the 3/8" wide red ribbon up along the top edge, with the ribbon extending slightly beyond the top of the interfacing. Hold in place with upright pins pushed through the ribbon into the ironing board padding. Set the iron on the lowest steam setting without steam and tack between the pins to secure the red ribbon, taking care not to touch the iron to the fusible.

    Butt the edge of the orange ribbon against the red, pin, and tack. Other colors follow in order. When all six colors are in place, fuse completely. I use a white tissue paper press cloth and the lowest setting for 10 seconds or less. Do not move the iron while fusing and work carefully. Ribbons and interfacing can shrink.

2. Use a card as a gauge to mark cutting lines 3 1/2" apart on the interfacing side of the fused strip. Cut on the lines. Cut the 1/4" ribbons into 12" lengths, mitering one end of each. With right side of ribbons to interfaced side of tube, pin and stitch as shown.

    Chaining: Feed one ribbon assembly after another into the machine, snipping the units apart later.

3. Bring the right sides of the tube together and join in a 1/4" seam, backstitching at both ends. These seams may also be chained.

4. Carefully turn the tube right side out and form a three-leg harness as shown using a needle and heavy-duty thread.

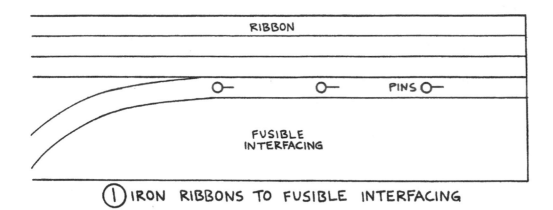

RIBBON

PINS

FUSIBLE
INTERFACING

① IRON RIBBONS TO FUSIBLE INTERFACING

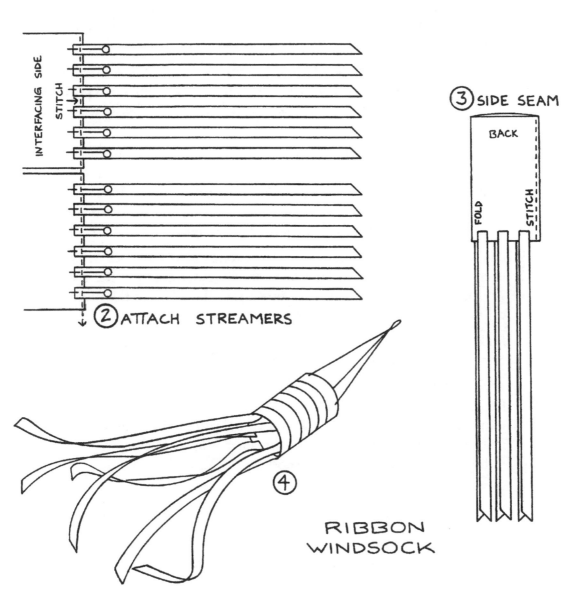

INTERFACING SIDE

STITCH

② ATTACH STREAMERS

③ SIDE SEAM

BACK

FOLD

STITCH

④

RIBBON
WINDSOCK

Fabric Windsock

Materials: sailcloth
24" plastic tubing 1/4" inner diameter
1/4" dia. dowel, 2" long
40" braided line, about 20#
large snap swivel
eyelets or tape for loops
reinforcements

A windsock with the length 2 1/2 times the diameter is a pleasing ratio. Streamers should be 2 1/2 times the length of the tube. The easy way is to cut them across the width of the material. Both streamers and tube may be pieced. This is a large windsock with a 25" tube.

Our pattern has six bands of color forming the tube. Of course, any color combination can be used. I have seen a white tube with an appliqued peacock and multi-colored streamers for the peacock tail. A band of Seminole quilting is another bright choice.

1.   Cut strips for the tube as shown with a sleeve allowance on the upper edge and a hem allowance on the lower. Cut six tails 4"-wide by the desired length. Hem the tails and finish the ends. Piece the tube, with 1/2" seams, pressing the seams flat and stitching the free edge down. The pieced panel will measure about 32"x26". Narrowly hem the bottom edge.

2-3.   Lay the right sides of the tails along the wrong side of the bottom edge. Space evenly, leaving 1/2" seam allowance on the outer edges of the tube. Stitch streamers in place. Right sides together, join the edges of the tube to form a cylinder (3).

Make the sleeve for the plastic tubing by turning 1/4" towards the wrong side on the top edge. Turn again 3/4" and stitch the sleeve, leaving an opening for insertion. Turn the tube right side out.

4.   Reinforce the windsock and insert eyelets as shown. Insert the tubing and join the ends with the dowel. With two 20" pieces of line and a snap swivel, make the harness as shown for the Streamer Windsock. Tangling is minimized if the windsock harness is fairly short.

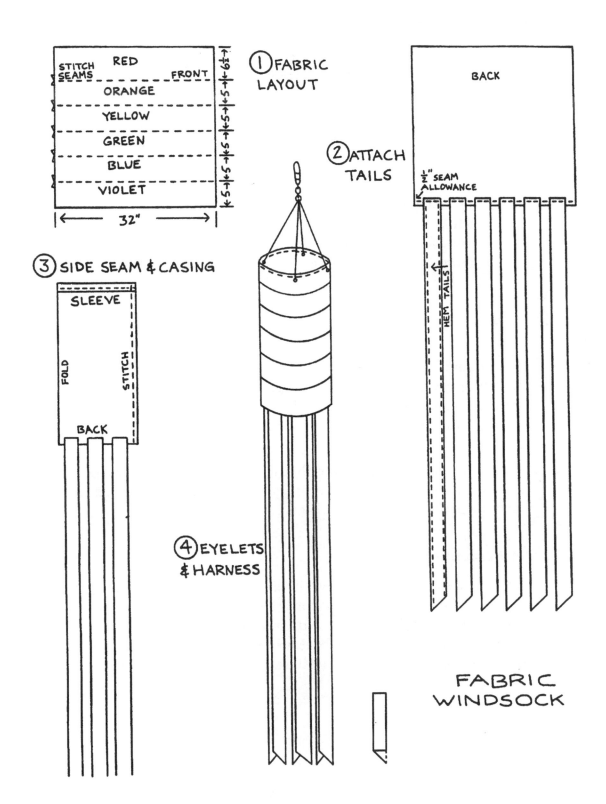

① FABRIC LAYOUT

RED
STITCH SEAMS   FRONT
ORANGE
YELLOW
GREEN
BLUE
VIOLET

32"

② ATTACH TAILS

BACK

½" SEAM ALLOWANCE

HEM TAILS

③ SIDE SEAM & CASING

SLEEVE
FOLD   STITCH
BACK

④ EYELETS & HARNESS

FABRIC
WINDSOCK

Plastic Parachute

Small parachutes are fun and use up good throwing energy in a safe way. For almost no cost, dozens of kids can be throwing objects into the air with all the force they can command. The result is parachutes blooming like flowers.

A little history: The first parachutes were unvented. The oscillation of an unvented canopy can cause the person or the payload to be dashed against the ground.

Materials: lightweight plastic, about 1 mil thick
cellophane tape
string for shroud lines
33mm film can for payload + small pebbles for weight
rubber band

Tools: scissors or sharp knife

1.   Draw a circle for the pattern, 16" in diameter being a good size. Use a pencil-and-string compass or draw around a large dishpan or tray. The plastic may be stacked with the pattern on top and several canopies cut at once with a sharp knife. Or trace around the pattern with a marking pen and cut out with scissors.

2-3.   Fold in half and fold again into thirds, trim the vent and mark segments as shown. Tape on the shroud lines and gather them together with a knot. Attach the payload with a rubber band.

Fabric Parachute

The circle should be at least 36" in diameter with a payload of appropriate weight. Large (6"-8") toy plastic figures may be just right. The weight is ideal when the parachute opens at the apex of the throw and descends slowly. If the pattern is cut into thirds or quarters, the canopy may be multi-colored. Hot cut the sailcloth and add loops or eyelets for the shroud lines.

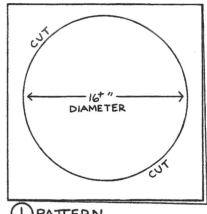

CUT

16^+ " DIAMETER

CUT

① PATTERN

PLASTIC PARACHUTE

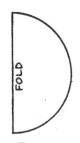

FOLD

FOLD

CUT $\frac{1}{2}$"

② FOLDING SEQUENCE

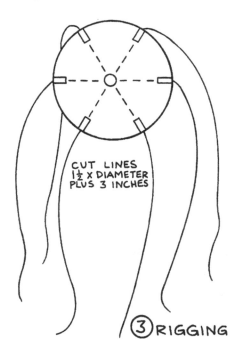

CUT LINES
1½ X DIAMETER
PLUS 3 INCHES

③ RIGGING

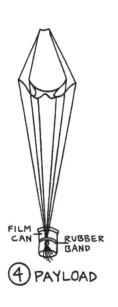

FILM CAN   RUBBER BAND

④ PAYLOAD

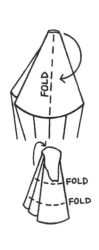

FOLD

FOLD

FOLD

Resources

A Few Kite Books

Greger, Margaret, *More Kites for Everyone,* 1990. 1425 Marshall, Richland, WA 99352. How-tos for 17 kites, including several new fabric designs.

Hart, Clive, *Kites, an Historical Survey,* Paul Appel, Mt. Vernon NY, 1982 (reprint of 1967 edition).

Pelham, David, *The Penguin Book of Kites,* (a reprint of the 1976 edition). Good historical reference and some patterns.

Thorburn, Neil, *Super Kites III,* 1991. 4738 Elmhurst Drive, San Jose, CA 95129. Creative deltas, boxes, sleds and combinations thereof, constructed of readily available, inexpensive materials.

Toy, Leland, *Flight Patterns,* 1984. Sunny Toy, 1718 Rex St., San Mateo, CA 94403. Eight simple kites.

Magazines and Newsletters

Kiting, quarterly journal of the American Kitefliers Association, PO Box 1614, Walla Walla, WA 99362. E-mail: aka@aka.kite.org. 800-252-2250 or 509-529-9171.

Drachen Foundation, 1907 Queen Anne Avenue North, Seattle, WA 98109. 206-282-4349. Fax: 206-284-5471. E-mail: info@drachen.org. A research center and repository for kite archives. Publishes a newsletter and curates exhibits around the world.

World Kite Museum & Hall of Fame, PO Box 964, Long Beach, WA 98631. E-mail: info@worldkitemuseum.com. 360-642-4020. Celebrates kiting through exhibits, classes for beginning and experienced kitemakers, demonstrations, and kite flying events. Publishes a quarterly newsletter.

Local kite clubs may also have newsletters.

Sources for Materials

The following listing is not exhaustive and does not include all that the various sources may have available.

Bear Packaging, 4265 Corporate Dr., Mt. Pleasant, MI 48858. 800-527-7189. mike@bearclaw.net. Large, bright-colored plastic bags, four colors to box of one hundred.

Gasworks Park Kite Shop, 3420 Stone Way North, Seattle, WA 98103. 206-633-4780. www.gasworksparkkiteshop.com. Catalog, kitemaking supplies, and books.

Great Winds Kite Co., 312 N. 83rd St., Seattle, WA 98103. Kitemaking supplies and books. Price list. www.greatwinds.com

Hang-em High Fabrics, 1420 Yale Ave., Richmond, VA 23224. 804-233-6155. www.citystar.com/hang-em-high

Into the Wind, 1408 Pearl St., Boulder, CA 80302. 800-541-1014. Color catalog of kites, kitemaking supplies, and books. www. intothewind.com

Kite Studio, 5555 Hamilton Blvd., Wescoville, PA 18106. 610-395-3560. Catalog, kitemaking supplies, books. www.kitebuilder.com

Saunders Brothers (West Coast Division), 1285 Bixby Drive, City of Industry, CA 91745. 800-421-9514. (East Coast Division) PO Box 1016, Westbrook, ME 04098. 800-343-0675. Dowels in quantity and at reasonable prices.

Kitelines Bookstore on line. 410-526-1033. Kitelinesbookstore.com. Lists and sells kite books from all over the world.

Index